The Village Youths and the Wealthy Banker

Zechariah Manyok Biar

ISBN: 9781764219341

Cover design, typesetting and layout: Africa World Books
Unit 3, 57 Frobisher St, Osborne Park, WA 6017
P.O. Box 1106 Osborne Park, WA 6916

Chapter One

In the land of Duomduom, a world far removed from modern cities and their luxuries, lies a village filled with the beauty of nature. The villagers in this rural paradise are blessed with lavish green pastures and authentic countryside huts that give a sense of belonging. As people from outside Duomduom begin their journey towards this village, they are greeted with the view of the Swamp of Dumkeer. The swamp's murky waters reflect the brilliant sunlight, creating an attractive view that is hard to miss.

Deep within, the village unfolds a captivating tapestry woven with the allure of the countryside. Tall grasses whisper secrets along meandering pathways, creating an enchanting entrance. Homes crowned with thatched grass roofs display a tender simplicity, stirring memories of bygone eras. This haven, a sanctuary from the frenzied pace of modern existence, offers respite and rejuvenation. A hidden jewel, it unveils itself gradually, a timeless realm where ancient charm persists. The village's charming character evokes a profound longing for a simpler life, one deeply rooted in the gentle sway of nature. Here, amidst the pastoral tranquillity, one finds solace, a refuge from the complexities of the contemporary world.

Rain transforms the village, painting it with the dazzling hues of butterflies. Their wings, exquisite blends of orange, lemon, and azure, dance amongst the luxuriant foliage, captivating the observer. At dawn and dusk, dragonflies, their bodies shimmering with delicate opalescence, become aerial predators. Their swift movements are a breathtaking dance of nature's artistry. The scene is one of unparalleled visual splendour.

Self-reliant and tenacious, the villagers coax sustenance from the rich soil, their existence inextricably bound to the natural world's pulse. For centuries, lives have blossomed and faded under the swamp's watchful gaze, their legacies indelibly imprinted on the land itself. A meandering trail edged with vibrant blooms and time-worn trees unveils the village.

As the villagers go about their daily routines, they are surrounded by the sounds of chirping birds and the gentle rustling of leaves. The air is filled with the sweet scent of wildflowers, which grow in abundance around the village. Technology has not yet made its way in, and the villagers rely on traditional ways of living. They are content with their way of life and have no desire for the modern amenities that city dwellers possess.

Nestled in the heart of the village, a tightly woven community thrives. Bound by deep kinship, villagers exhibit unwavering mutual support, mirroring a familial devotion. Just as a bird's nest provides shelter for its inhabitants, this community protects and nurtures its own similarly. Their close-knit bonds are the foundation of their strength and unity.

A rich tapestry of ancestral customs, meticulously guarded across countless years, finds vibrant expression in their spirited festivals. The bonfire's comforting glow symbolises the deep bonds uniting their close-knit society. Age-old narratives, brimming with profound wisdom and captivating magic, mould the identities of their youth. This invaluable cultural legacy constitutes their most prized possession.

The villagers' lives revolve around their cattle, which serve as the foundation of their economy. These animals play a vital role in providing them with sustenance and resources, making them indispensable to their survival. The village is dotted with camps, each with its distinct layout, reflecting the villagers' reliance on their cattle for all aspects of life. Despite their limited means, the villagers' resourcefulness is apparent in the rudimentary tents and fences scattered throughout the village.

More than mere livestock, their cattle embody a profound ancestral heritage, a legacy meticulously preserved across generations. Their lives pulse with the rhythm of tending these animals—a ceaseless cycle of milking, pasture management, and vigilant guardianship. Each family's dwelling, a proof of ingenuity and necessity, contributes to a dynamic panorama of temporary homes. Young ones frolic amongst the grazing herds, absorbing the wisdom of their forefathers. This seemingly uncomplicated existence masks an unwavering tenacity honed by years of confronting an unforgiving landscape.

Life unfolds languidly for them, governed by the sun's relentless journey and the demands of their animals. Rudimentary implements and age-old techniques shape their days. A profound serenity emanates from their self-reliance, a stark juxtaposition to the frenetic pace of the modern world. Deep camaraderie binds this close-knit community, forged in shared toil and modest pleasures. Yet, this pleasant haven is jeopardised by the insidious creep of external development, a looming threat to their peaceful existence. The fate of their tranquil way of life hangs precariously in the scales of an uncertain future.

Despite the challenges they face, the villagers take pride in their cattle and their way of life. It is a world that is filled with its unique charm and beauty, one that is often overlooked by the modern world. The cattle camps serve as a reminder of the villagers' resilience and their ability to find joy and contentment in the simplest of things. It is a world that may seem primitive to some, but for the villagers, it is their home and their way of life.

What makes this sight even more enchanting is the unique spectacle that unfolds during the dry season. As the swamp's water levels recede, the cattle camps scatter throughout the village and move closer to the edge of the swamp. This creates a breathtaking view as the cattle graze and the makeshift tents and fences come into full view.

A symphony of nocturnal sounds—the resonant croaks of frogs, the insistent chirps of crickets, and the deep-throated mooing of cattle—paints a vivid soundscape over the village. This nightly concert makes a significant contribution to the village's serene atmosphere. The normally crucial cattle enclosures now play a vital role, supplying crucial nourishment to the surge of festival-goers. The upcoming seasonal festivities magnify their significance. This exquisite fusion of natural beauty and community spirit promises a spectacular celebration, exponentially increasing the village's allure.

The dry season, a relentless adversary, paradoxically forges deeper connections within these communities. Facing shared hardships, neighbours intertwine, their mutual dependence strengthening the fabric of their society. Their collective efforts ensure the survival of their livestock, demonstrating their unwavering resolve. This ordeal of adversity refines their spirit, cultivating resilience and a great sense of unity. Even amidst the stark desolation, their laughter rings out, a vibrant counterpoint to the arid landscape, symbolising their indomitable spirit.

The advancing dry season transforms Duomduom village into a sun-drenched paradise. The radiant sun and azure expanse above complete the pleasant picture, a sanctuary removed from global turmoil and strife. In this serene interlude, the villagers deeply savour the unblemished charm and tranquil elegance of their secluded rural retreat.

Moreover, the dry season yields a captivating aroma from the cattle encampment, a fragrance as potent as any visual spectacle. The rich, earthy scent of manure blends harmoniously with the soothing aroma of dried grass, a distinctive perfume decipherable only to those intimately familiar with the camp's nocturnal atmosphere. As twilight descends, painting the heavens with a myriad of twinkling stars, a tranquil cadence settles over the encampment. Untethered, young calves exuberantly jostle one another, their boundless energy a stark contrast to the placid repose of the mature cattle, who, weary from their day's foraging, rest in silent contentment. It is a scene that profoundly evokes a life both unassuming and deeply satisfying.

The villagers take immense pride in their cattle enclosures, pouring their hearts and souls into their upkeep. These enclosures demonstrate their tireless efforts and determination to thrive in a harsh environment. The meticulous arrangement of the enclosures speaks volumes about the villagers' unwavering dedication and resilience. The rugged walls serve as a reminder of their strong connection to nature, while the sturdy wooden beams and cow-dung-coated roofs offer a sense of security and comfort. Each worn and weathered surface holds a wealth of memories, serving as the foundation of the villagers' livelihoods.

For centuries, the people of Duomduom have shared an intimate existence with their herds, their lives interwoven with the rhythms of the cattle pens. The pervasive aroma, deeply embedded in their collective memory, is a tangible symbol of their shared prosperity and social fabric. This profound interdependence has moulded their customs and beliefs, creating a unique cultural legacy. The very atmosphere of Duomduom resonates with the echoes of generations past, a powerful narrative etched in the lives of both humans and animals, a poignant illustration of their unwavering bond.

Within the enclosure, the camp's elders often convene, their voices resonating through the stillness of the night as they deliberate on decisions shaping the collective destiny. This hallowed space pulses with significance; even the young calves tethered near its boundary seem to sense its profound importance, their gazes fixed upon it with an almost wistful yearning.

In Duomduom, the cattle kraals are the very essence of the villagers' lives, transcending mere practicality. More than mosquito protection for their herds, these meticulously crafted enclosures demonstrate the villagers' unyielding dedication and tireless industry. They are not simply a lifeline but a powerful symbol of their profound and enduring kinship with the earth.

Within the cattle encampment, life unfolds at a relaxed pace. Even the youngest inhabitants often stay awake until late at night, only to rise with the sun's gentle ascent. Following the evening milking time of the cows, a vibrant chorus would emerge from excited singers, their voices weaving a captivating melody around the perimeter of the settlement, extending far into the night. Children, captivated, trail joyfully behind the singers, while women and elders, comfortably nestled within their shelters, would listen with serene contentment to the enchanting strains. This nighttime symphony, a deeply ingrained cultural ritual, significantly contributes to the inhabitants' leisurely sleep patterns.

As the morning mist dissipates, the camp comes alive with a flurry of activity. The young boys and girls, eager to prove their worth, are assigned their daily responsibilities of tending to the cows. The older girls and boys are entrusted with the crucial task of milking the cows. As the sun continues to rise, the women of the camp, known for their early rises, gather to engage in various activities.

As the morning progresses, the men of the camp join in on the daily tasks. The men, known for their strength and resilience, are responsible for leading the cows to the pastures. With their expertise and knowledge, they guide the herd to the lush green fields, ensuring that the cows are well-fed and taken care of. The entire community works together in harmony, with each member playing a vital role in the camp's daily functioning.

The cowherders' days are long and filled with hard work. Nevertheless, they maintain their spirits by finding beauty in even the most mundane tasks. When the cattle go to the pastures and the bright sun illuminates the vast fields, the cowherders carefully scatter cow dung in unique ways, transforming a practical chore into a breathtaking spectacle. Each meticulously placed pat becomes not merely fuel for their evening fires, but a tribute to their artistic spirit —a vibrant expression born from the heart of their humble existence.

The dried dung serves as a source of fuel for the evening fires, providing warmth and smoke for the villagers. The neatly stacked dung has a faint aroma that reminds the villagers of their cattle camps' lifestyle. Its rough texture and crumbling edges testify to its age and use. It also exhibits a subtle, earthy fragrance, a poignant reminder of the villagers' agrarian heritage. The cheerful crackle and snap of the flames gradually consume the dried dung, generously dispensing warmth – a comforting, nightly ritual in the villagers' simple existence.

A thick, acrid smoke, born from the burning dung, hangs heavy in the air, shrouding the landscape in a spectral haze. This seemingly bizarre practice, far from being arbitrary, offers vital protection to the herd. The pungent fumes act as a powerful deterrent, shielding the cattle from the swarms of voracious mosquitoes that infest the parched wetlands during the harsh heat of the dry season.

The livestock camp is a sight to behold. Children run around, laughter filling the air, while the women cook and chat. Men stand guard, their presence commanding respect. The camp is often bustling with life. The children's gleeful shouts and the women's chatter merge with the men's watchful voices. The animals add to the liveliness, their bleating and mooing blending with the hum of activity.

As twilight descends, the air vibrates with mirth, and the resonant voices recount timeless stories. Communal feasts deepen the bonds of fellowship, while the sage pronouncements of the elders illuminate the path for their successors, ensuring the enduring legacy of their culture. Tales of valour and adversity instil unwavering optimism, forging a powerful sense of unity through this nightly ceremony. This cherished tradition steels their resolve, empowering them to face the uncertainties of the morrow. The anticipation of their next reunion hangs noticeably in the air, a demonstration of its profound importance.

Like moths drawn to a flame, the camp residents are drawn to this sacred moment, basking in the comfort and familiarity it brings. As the fire burns on, so does their connection to each other and their beloved community. The flickering flames act as a beacon, guiding the villagers towards each other and fostering a deep sense of belonging. As they gather around the fire, they are enveloped in a warm embrace, a reminder of the enduring bonds that hold them together. The fire becomes a symbol of their unity, a source of strength and comfort, bringing them closer together like a family.

A profound sense of equilibrium prevails in the cattle camp. It is a place of harmony where individuals collaborate in unison with nature and one another. A strong sense of camaraderie pervades every aspect of daily life, from communal meals to collective efforts in maintaining the camp. While the outside world is filled with chaos, the cattle camp serves as a tranquil refuge.

Through shared endeavours ranging from sustenance gathering to constructing makeshift homes, campers synergistically leverage their unique proficiencies. This collective exertion cultivates profound camaraderie and reciprocal admiration. The immersive experience forges enduring connections, vividly illustrating the potency of teamwork in conquering adversity. The serene majesty of the natural landscape serves as a harmonious backdrop, amplifying their unified spirit. This collaborative ethos, nurtured within nature's embrace, promises to enrich individual lives and propel future achievements in the broader society. A future brimming with further expeditions awaits, built upon this strengthened foundation of shared accomplishment.

In the cattle camp, a vibrant tapestry of cultures intertwines as shared meals and joyous laughter forge unlikely bonds. A powerful sense of community blossoms from their mutual reliance, creating a haven of belonging where each individual feels deeply connected. This immersive experience cultivates overwhelming empathy and collaborative spirit, imparting invaluable life lessons that extend far beyond the camp's confines. The atmosphere crackles with positive energy, a vibrant demonstration of their unified endeavour. The camp's enduring influence extends far beyond its physical location; it plants seeds of harmony and mutual understanding that promise to cultivate a more compassionate and interconnected world. The enduring legacy of this shared experience heralds a future filled with hope and promise.

In Duomduom, cattle are far more than a financial asset; they are the very cornerstone of the village's social order. Protecting the precious herd serves as a rigorous rite of passage, a crucible where boys prove their mettle, fostering both spirited rivalry and enduring friendships. This deeply ingrained hierarchy, its roots firmly planted in cattle husbandry, mirrors the village's power structure and foreshadows future leadership roles. Seasoned youths guide their less experienced counterparts, imparting vital skills essential for survival. A young man's prowess in this demanding environment directly dictates his future prominence, shaping his trajectory within the community. Thus, the village's future leaders are moulded, tempered, and tested amidst the grime and exertion of the cattle enclosures.

Beyond their utilitarian purpose, the cattle pens evolve into a powerful emblem of the boys' burgeoning friendships. These enclosures, initially mere holding areas for livestock, transcend their practical function, becoming havens where the tedium of village existence yields to the vibrant tapestry of shared experiences and youthful camaraderie. Here, amidst the lowing cattle, a profound sense of kinship blossoms as the boys forge unbreakable bonds, finding solace and strength in mutual support. The pens are no longer simply functional spaces; they are transformed into sacred ground, a refuge where the daily grind melts away, replaced by the enduring warmth of genuine connection.

The relaxing image of village life belied a stark reality: profound heterogeneity. Nhomlaau town, for instance, presented a lifestyle dramatically different from that of Duomduom village. A striking divergence lay in the inhabitants' vigorous preventative measures against the relentless onslaught of disease-carrying mosquitoes in Nhomlaau.

The pristine beauty of Duomduom, once held sacred, began

to fade under the corrosive weight of a desire for security and comfort. The absence of medical care in Duomduom cast a long shadow, profoundly altering the villagers' perspectives and threatening their collective well-being. A demonstrable sense of foreboding settled upon their future. Responding to this crisis, the Nhomlaau mayor initiated a program to deliver vital healthcare services to the Duomduom community.

A doctor from Nhomlaau, Dr. Jameson, emphasising the stark disparity between the two communities, meticulously instructed the Duomduom villagers on the insidious source of their children's ailments: mosquito-borne diseases. He powerfully demonstrated that the most potent defence employed in Nhomlaau – the use of cow dung smoke as a protective barrier within the spacious cattle enclosures – offered a critical advantage. This effective, albeit rudimentary, method, unavailable in their cramped dwellings, was presented as a crucial intervention. He passionately advocated for its adoption within their homes, urging them to replicate this life-saving practice.

While the physical beauty of Duomduom was always appreciated, some now see the irresistible allure of Nhomlaau. The opulence of Nhomlaau's majestic mansions stood in stark, previously unappreciated contrast to the modest abodes of Duomduom. Nhomlaau's prosperity overflowed, evidenced by its bountiful harvests. This newfound affluence facilitated a thrice-daily meal, a privilege unimaginable in the less privileged Duomduom. The ubiquitous mosquito netting within Nhomlaau's opulent residences further underscored their superior lifestyle.

Town dwellers in Nhomlaau enjoyed a starkly different existence from their rural counterparts. Privileged access to education, healthcare, and essential provisions afforded them a standard of living unimaginable to the villagers in Duomduom. The town, nestled amidst luxuriant hills and abundant foliage, boasted a breathtaking panorama dominated by imposing castles. A life-giving river, meandering nearby, furnished both potable water and richly productive farmland, fostering a prosperous and self-sustaining community.

Nhomlaau's fragrant gardens, overflowing with a riotous profusion of blossoms, were integral to the town's distinctive character. Every dwelling showcased its own meticulously tended patch, a powerful symbol of communal harmony and personal accomplishment. These lovingly cultivated flowers served not merely as adornment; they yielded vital herbs and medicinal plants, enhancing the townspeople's well-being. This deep connection fostered a profound bond between the residents and their verdant surroundings. The town's visionary leaders, with their farsighted wisdom, guaranteed that future growth would not diminish this precious aromatic legacy, proactively incorporating ample space for flourishing gardens.

While Nhomlaau town could battle poverty occasionally on a class basis, Duomduom village as a whole would occasionally cling precariously to existence, a community ravaged by despair. Their wretched circumstances would exact a terrible price, leaving an indelible mark on their health. Children would sometimes gasp for breath, their tiny bodies wracked by relentless coughing fits; adults would be crippled by chronic ailments, their vitality sapped. Persistent famines would gnaw at their dwindling reserves, pushing them to the precipice of starvation. Erratic harvests would repeatedly plunge families into abject impoverishment, their hopes shattered by unrelenting adversity. The ever-present threat of famine would often loom, a grim harbinger of unending misery, casting a cloud of hopelessness over their bleak future.

However, Duomduom underwent a profound transformation,

spurred by the doctor's regular presence. Nhomlaau's revolutionary healthcare initiatives sparked a remarkable evolution. Sturdy, improved homes supplanted crumbling huts; vibrant, malaria-deterrent bed nets offered enhanced protection; and a nourishing diet fostered renewed vitality. This invigorating revival instilled a deep and pervasive sense of communal pride within the village.

The doctor's visits not only brought medical aid but also ignited hope in the people of Duomduom, a hope for a brighter future. Sanitation and hygiene improvements revolutionised Duomduom, drastically curtailing the incidence of infectious diseases. Children, previously burdened by illness, began to experience a remarkable surge in well-being. This physical transformation was deeply intertwined with a burgeoning community spirit. Collaboration and self-sufficiency began to thrive, creating a powerful sense of collective agency. This newfound empowerment fuelled a cascade of positive developments within the village.

However, as the town's economy continued to prosper, the gap between Nhomlaau and Duomduom seemed to widen. Nhomlaau's burgeoning wealth dramatically improved its healthcare and educational systems, leaving Duomduom in a state of relative deprivation. This widening gap reproduced bitter animosity and simmering conflict between the adjacent communities. The stark divergence in living standards carved a deep societal rift, permeating every aspect of life, from mundane routines to the exercise of political power. Duomduom's inhabitants felt increasingly marginalised and forgotten. Their pleas for assistance were ignored. This escalating inequality posed a grave threat to regional stability, prompting urgent questions about equitable resource distribution and the pursuit of sustainable progress. The future hung precariously in the balance.

Despite their glaring differences, Nhomlaau and Duomduom

were not always so vastly unequal. They were once on equal footing, with a symbiotic relationship that benefited both communities. However, as the years went on, Nhomlaau's economy flourished while Duomduom's stagnated. This growing disparity between the "haves" and the "have-nots" has left a deep rift between the two communities, sparking a tale of two worlds with no end in sight.

Nhomlaau's transformation stemmed from an influx of international entrepreneurs, flush with capital and innovative ventures. Finding Nhomlaau a secure haven for investment, they fuelled the town's explosive growth. This entrepreneurial spirit proved contagious. Residents embraced commerce, propelling Nhomlaau's prosperity. In stark contrast, Duomduom's resistance to outside influences condemned it to stagnation, a stark proof of the transformative power of embracing global engagement.

For generations, Nhomlaau's aristocratic clans had been integral to the town's exquisite upkeep, meticulously safeguarding its legacy and making substantial contributions to its splendour. The town's impeccably maintained infrastructure boasted a sophisticated drainage system, expertly engineered to eliminate stagnant pools—breeding grounds for disease-carrying insects. This meticulous urban planning resulted in an atmosphere refreshingly devoid of the fetid odours of decay, creating a hygienic and delightful environment for its inhabitants. The captivating aroma of Nhomlaau was more than a mere fragrance; it embodied the town's inherent beauty, rich cultural tapestry, and the unwavering pride of its citizens.

The town of Nhomlaau was a wondrous sight to behold. The streets were lined with vibrant gardens, full of colourful flowers and lush greenery. The homes were a mix of traditional and modern architecture, creating a blend of past and present. The people, with their warm smiles and welcoming gestures, made visitors feel at ease. As you walked through the town, you could see the strong sense of community that bound its residents together. The locals worked together to maintain the town's cleanliness and beauty, with every street corner adorned with artwork and paintings. The overall atmosphere was one of peace and contentment, a reflection of the town's values of selflessness and harmony.

Nhomlaau's allure and captivating atmosphere mesmerised all who visited. The streets were teeming with amiable locals going about their daily routines. The air was filled with tantalising scents of delectable cuisine and the delightful sound of laughter and chatter, creating an irresistible atmosphere. The inviting warmth and mouthwatering fare of the town welcome visitors from far and wide, eager to immerse themselves in the ways of its inhabitants and their unique lifestyle. Nhomlaau's attractive streets and hospitable people made it an essential destination for those seeking a glimpse into its distinct culture.

Nhomlaau's market was a mixture of sights and smells, bursting with the intoxicating perfume of exotic fruits and pungent spices interwoven with the savoury fragrance of sizzling meats. Skilled Nhomlaau artisans proudly exhibited their exquisite, handcrafted treasures, each piece a testament to the town's rich and singular cultural legacy. A mesmerising fusion of age-old customs and contemporary ingenuity created a beguiling environment. This captivating synthesis of past and present promised a transformative journey for those courageous enough to unravel Nhomlaau's unfathomable secrets and hidden narratives.

Nhomlaau's inhabitants enthusiastically embraced sharing their rich cultural heritage. Their lavish, thrice-daily feasts, welcoming both villagers and strangers into a vibrant celebration, demonstrated this open-heartedness. This deeply ingrained communal practice not only fortified the settlement's social fabric but also powerfully underscored its reputation for inclusivity and unparalleled generosity.

The residents of Nhomlaau were skilled in various forms of medicine, often providing healthcare assistance to the villagers in need. Their medical prowess transcended rudimentary healthcare. They commanded sophisticated expertise in herbal medicine and delivered skilled midwifery services. This comprehensive approach to wellness fostered a flourishing community. These esteemed families also acted as profound patrons of the arts, commissioning breathtaking works and nurturing local artisans. Their cultural patronage infused the villagers' lives with vibrancy, cultivating a powerful sense of shared identity and collective purpose.

However, the sublime façade of Nhomlaau concealed a predatory scheme against the unsuspecting inhabitants of Duomduom. Nhomlaau's prosperity, deceptively built on a foundation of guile, stemmed from the surreptitious exploitation of Duomduom's resources. Their guileful neighbours clandestinely pilfered the milk from Duomduom's peacefully grazing herds, a callous theft masked by outward friendship. Furthermore, Nhomlaau's residents ravenously consumed Duomduom's rich land and bountiful waters, heedless of the devastating ecological consequences. This rapacious behaviour resulted in the impoverishment of Duomduom's natural wealth and inflicted grievous damage upon the fragile ecosystem.

Duomduom's inhabitants, previously sheltered in blissful unawareness, were cruelly awakened to Nhomlaau's deceptive nature. The veneer of perfection shattered, revealing a stark and unsettling truth. The town's illustrious reputation, once a blinding beacon, now served only to underscore the depth of the concealed depravity. Confronted with this long-hidden reality, the people of Duomduom were forced to confront a bitter and agonising disillusionment.

Chapter Two

The Duomduom cattle camps, once a flourishing paradise, now faced a looming threat. The villagers were troubled by the dwindling milk production of their once-robust cows. Like a vibrant painting marred by a dark stain, the lush green pastures were tainted by this troubling problem. Duomduom's livestock and children were at risk.

The villagers' lives were profoundly interwoven with their cattle. These animals were not merely a source of food but the very embodiment of their wealth and cultural identity. As steadfast as their unwavering herds, the villagers had always weathered hardship. However, a devastating crisis loomed: a precipitous decline in milk production, hinting at a sinister exploitation preying upon their beloved animals. This dwindling supply wasn't just a nutritional deficiency; it signified a catastrophic weakening, a draining of their people's life dynamism. A profound chill gripped the villagers. The ancient bond between them and their animals was fracturing, a calamitous unravelling of their shared heritage.

Faced with this dilemma, the villagers turned to their trusted traditional healer, a sorcerer whose words were like divine guidance. They relied on him for years for their survival. However, for the first time, even the healer seemed uncertain. As a result, the villagers were in a state of bewilderment, with no apparent solution in sight.

The healer, his normally confident countenance creased with uncertainty, consulted his sacred spear for direction. His visible distress amplified the villagers' terror, a frigid wave of fear engulfing the terrified populace. Whispers of a forgotten ritual, a last desperate gamble against the encroaching shadows, spread like wildfire. This ancient rite required a singular, rare plant, rumoured to flourish only in the treacherous depths of the Duomduom jungle. Despite the freezing grip of dread tightening their hearts, the villagers resolved to undertake the perilous trip, their lives—and faith in the ritual's power—hanging by a thread.

A courageous party of ten youths, accompanied by the village soothsayer, ventured deep into the emerald labyrinth of the jungle. Their perilous mission was to procure the sacred herb essential for the mystical rite of divination. After three arduous hours, they emerged triumphantly bearing the coveted plant.

A wave of fervent anticipation surged through the village. Nearly every inhabitant poured forth, a surging tide of hope and anxiety, to witness the unfolding prophecy. The community yearned for answers to the ominous decline in their cattle's milk production, a crisis threatening their very livelihood.

A crowd of anxious villagers, their features etched with apprehension, awaited the pronouncements of their revered medicine man. His gristly appearance and intense gaze usually radiated an air of profound knowledge, a near-sacred authority. Nonetheless, an unprecedented uncertainty clouded his pronouncements, leaving the community stunned and adrift. Hope flickered in their upturned faces, yet the healer offered no solace, no path forward.

The crisis intensified with each passing day. The villagers' existence hung precariously on the usual abundant yield of their dairy herds. Deprived of this sustenance, a devastating famine loomed. The urgency of finding a remedy was stark; their very survival, the continued existence of their community, was at stake.

A profound uncertainty gripped the community. Its destiny hung precariously in the balance. The urgency of finding a resolution pressed heavily upon them, a stark awareness of dwindling time fuelling their anxiety. Gazing upon their verdant pastures and the listless cattle, they succumbed to a gnawing despair. Their plight resembled a vessel adrift, becalmed in a sea of indecision. A panorama of potential opportunities stretched before them, yet paralysis held them captive. The lush fields and unproductive livestock served only as a constant, crushing reminder of their stagnation.

For generations, the people of Duomduom had depended on agriculture and their livestock for sustenance. Their fields now flourished, vibrant and luxuriant, yet a grim paradox emerged: the yield of milk from their healthy, well-fed cattle steadily decreased. Faced with this disheartening decline, the villagers, resolute in their purpose, were determined to overcome this adversity and restore their community's prosperity.

Duomduom's elders were profoundly apprehensive that their children's deteriorating health might prompt unwanted intervention from neighbouring Nhomlaau. This prospect was deeply unsettling, a stark violation of their fiercely guarded independence and self-sufficiency. Their traditional pride in autonomy lay shattered, and they were utterly vulnerable to the capricious whims of nature. While medical intervention was grudgingly acceptable, the villagers resolutely rejected any form of food relief, clinging fiercely to their dignity.

Driven by desperation, several respected community members proposed a desperate measure: a second consultation with the enigmatic sorcerer. His initial pronouncements regarding the afflicted cattle and their dwindling milk yield had proven utterly inadequate. The others, swayed by this compelling argument, readily concurred. Their return to the sorcerer's dwelling was accompanied by a significantly increased offering, demonstrating their growing anxiety and the gravity of the situation.

Driven by the villagers' deepening agony and hopelessness, the healer resolved to enhance his prophetic abilities. Though weighed down by the immense responsibility, he embarked upon his divination, desperately seeking insight and solace to unravel the community's plight.

A muted reverence fell over the elders as the sorcerer plunged into a profound meditative state. Their gaze, unwavering and expectant, tracked his every subtle gesture. A substantial impression of urgency, of finality, hung in the air. This was their ultimate recourse. With each drawn-out breath, the sorcerer's communion with the ethereal realm intensified, culminating in a vision that offered a strategy for survival.

The sorcerer paused for a few minutes; his gaze locked on a celestial phenomenon unseen by the others. A wave of awe, then terror, washed over the village elders as he began rituals of unimaginable scope and brutality—a horrifying display of might and appeasement surpassing all previous experience. From him radiated an intense energy, a dazzling promise of salvation from their desperate predicament.

A palpable thrum of ancient incantations vibrated through the sorcerer's compound, igniting a fragile spark of hope in the elders' exhausted eyes. With practised fluidity, his fingers danced, conjuring luminous glyphs that shimmered in the twilight. Unseen energies surged, crackling like a storm about to break. The crux of the villagers' desperate fight rested upon a seldom-employed, sacred plant—its potent tincture heralded a potential turning of the tide.

Despite the healer's best efforts, nothing seemed to change, but the healer was not ready to give up. He knew that sometimes, the spirits worked in mysterious ways, and he was determined to keep. With renewed determination, he called upon the spirits once again, hoping that this time, they would hear his plea and restore the milk production to the village.

Still, nothing changed. Days turned into weeks; the decreased milk from the cattle of Duomduom was a constant source of anxiety in the entire village. The sorcerer's magical abilities seemed useless against this mundane problem. His frustration mounted, threatening to overwhelm his usual calm demeanour.

As the weeks passed without any tangible results, the villagers continued to grapple with this unexpected crisis. Some had conducted their research, observing the cattle's behaviour and diet in hopes of finding a solution. Others had turned to neighbouring villages for assistance, seeking advice and support.

A frenzy of outrageous gossip consumed the villagers. Accusations flew like poisoned darts; some whispered of a neighbouring clan's malicious curse on their livestock, while others cited celestial malice as the culprit. With their dairy yields plummeting, the community found itself adrift in a sea of apprehension, their future as bleak and uncertain as a starless night.

A resolute assembly of villagers convened, their faces etched with grim purpose. United by a shared urgency, they sought to diagnose the affliction plaguing their community and wrestle it from the jaws of impending doom. Their collective resolve burned bright as they dug deep into the heart of the problem, their determined gaze fixed on a future they intended to forge anew. With unwavering conviction, they embark on a quest to unearth the source of their village's suffering and secure its survival against an uncertain destiny.

It was now evident that a calamitous predicament gripped the village, demanding immediate action. The crisis, an inescapable force, threatened to squash them. They were compelled to rally, to bolster one another against its weight. As gravity binds all matter, so too must they forge a unified response, their collective strength the only counterweight to impending disaster.

Facing a desperate need for information, the villagers deliberated. Their collective decision was to navigate the bustling Nhomlaau marketplace, the economic heart of their region. This was no mere shopping trip. It was a calculated foray, a bold expedition into a complex commercial arena. Like seasoned explorers charting uncharted waters, they embraced the inherent risks, their resolve hardened by the vital intelligence they sought. The market's intricate dynamics presented a formidable challenge, one they were determined to conquer with unwavering courage and strategic prowess.

Following extensive deliberation, the villagers devised a daring scheme: to infiltrate the marketplace disguised as milk purchasers. The inherent perils were considerable. Yet, the community's determination to secure vital intelligence proved unwavering, compelling them to embrace the substantial risk.

The group faced many challenges during their mission, but the main difficulty was the language barrier. None of them spoke the language that many business people spoke in Nhomlaau town, making it almost impossible to gather helpful information. The local vendors met them with confusion and suspicion.

The group was growing frustrated and ready to call it quits. After several days of failed attempts, the group decided to seek help from a translator. As fate would have it, the translator was a native of their neighbouring village. With the translator's help, the group was finally able to communicate with the townspeople and gather more information about the milk. They learned that the milk was being supplied by a group of mysterious nomads who came to the village once a month to sell their products. Who were these nomads, and why were they supplying milk to the town?

The deeper the investigators probed, the more impenetrable the mystery became. No corroborating proof emerged to support the itinerant tribe's narrative, leaving the detectives to suspect a phantom fabrication, a cunning deception designed to mislead their inquiry.

Despite lacking formal training in criminal investigation, the villagers conducted their inquiry with remarkable diligence. Each minuscule clue was rigorously scrutinised, and no detail escaped their meticulous examination in the relentless pursuit of justice. Undeterred by seemingly insurmountable obstacles, their resolve to expose the truth and silence the doubters burned fiercely.

Driven by a profound personal commitment that far exceeded mere duty, the village investigators relentlessly pursued evidence of the nomadic tribe's whereabouts. Their quest, a dogged and unwavering resolve to unravel this enigma completely, echoed in the desolate silence of the empty thoroughfares. With meticulous intensity, they scoured every hidden recess, their minds laser-focused on achieving their definitive solution.

Some days into their inquiry, the investigators were profoundly perplexed. They discovered that the milk vendors were ordinary townsfolk—a baffling revelation. The sheer volume of milk, its monthly delivery, and its remarkable preservation throughout the month defied comprehension. How could nomadic tribes procure and transport such quantities? The investigators found themselves grappling with an enigma, the inexplicable source of Nhomlaau's milk supply, a source of intense frustration and bewilderment.

A Duomduom investigator had strong suspicions that Nhomlaau's business owners were clandestinely milking their cattle during the daytime, during the grazing hours, within the secluded woodland. Subsequently, they transported the illicit dairy products to the town under the cover of darkness. To ascertain the veracity of these allegations, the investigative unit conducted a rigorous three-day covert operation, meticulously shadowing the herd throughout their grazing period. This intensive monitoring aimed to expose any clandestine activities definitively and gather irrefutable evidence.

The news of the secretive operation rapidly spread among the undercover milk thieves through a system of spies within the town, who had been monitoring the Duomduom team. This discovery led to an immediate halt in their illicit activities, resulting in a significant increase in milk production at the cattle camp.

Duomduom village was gripped by astonishment when an unforeseen explosion in milk yields from their local dairy farm left them utterly perplexed. What had once been a threatening situation was suddenly awash with frenetic energy, a bewildering transformation that sparked fervent debate and speculation. Some posited a celestial hand in this extraordinary event; others whispered of a sacred occurrence.

After three arduous days of pursuing the herd through dense bush, the investigative team, based in a neighbouring hamlet, made the strategic decision to shift their operational base to Nhomlaau town at nightfall on the third day. Rumours of a significant surge in milk production in the village of Duomduom spurred their relocation. However, the team remained profoundly unaware of the unfolding situation in the Nhomlaau marketplace, lacking any local intelligence to gauge the volume of milk traded there.

On the fourth day of their return to town, the investigators revisited the market and were met with milk merchants selling their goods. However, as the day turned to night, they realised that the milk supply in Duomduom villages had decreased once again. This led them to infer that the townspeople were responsible for milking the cows. Despite their allegations, the investigators lacked solid evidence to support them.

As most of the population depended on the chosen investigators, any information about what happened in their absence remained a mystery. With no one to turn to, the villagers were at the mercy of the investigators, who were chosen to represent them. They were left to wonder and speculate about what could have possibly happened during their absence.

The investigative team's ill-conceived plan to clandestinely track the cattle through the dense bush backfired spectacularly. Their failure to divide their forces left them utterly blind to events unfolding simultaneously in the bustling Nhomlaau marketplace. This flawed strategy yielded no practical intelligence; their painstaking pursuit only revealed the unremarkable truth that the cows were not milked.

Their ambitious attempt to achieve dual objectives proved disastrously inefficient. It was a futile exercise akin to grasping at shadows. Instead of a comprehensive understanding, they gained nothing. A more focused, sequential approach—addressing each investigative thread individually—would have yielded far superior results. Their blunder serves as a stark reminder of the pitfalls of attempting to handle multiple complex tasks concurrently. It is a classic example of diluted efforts producing meagre outcomes.

Driven by a profound sense of urgency, the investigators resolved to disclose their disturbing suspicions to the town's mayor, hoping to illuminate the city's festering underbelly. The mayor's office, a sanctuary of integrity, offered a lifeline amidst the treacherous currents of corruption and duplicity. With unwavering faith, they relied on the mayor's sagacity to steer them toward the elusive truth.

The town's mayor responded to the request by summoning a gathering and conveying the allegation to the town's residents. However, the townsfolk refuted any involvement in milking cows at the nearby village of Duomduom. They demanded a retraction from the villagers, whom they accused of besmirching their reputation. They issued a warning that they would prohibit the villagers from entering the town unless an apology was given promptly.

However, the Duomduom people harboured an unshakeable belief in the townspeople's guilt, a conviction that transcended the lack of tangible proof presented to Nhomlaau's mayor. For them, the accusation wasn't merely a suspicion. It was a certainty, a damning indictment despite the absence of irrefutable evidence.

This unwavering stance sparked a furious backlash among some villagers and townspeople. The villagers strongly rejected the townspeople's demands for an apology. Bound by their conscience, they felt an inescapable moral obligation to confront the pervasive injustices plaguing the villagers of Duomduom, regardless of the personal cost.

Nevertheless, the villagers were quite aware of the consequences of their actions. They knew that the townspeople were powerful and could retaliate against them for exposing the truth. They also knew that they could not continue living in fear and ignorance. They had to take a stand and fight for justice, even if it meant facing the wrath of the powerful townspeople.

Facing a formidable and perilous undertaking, the villagers resolved to persevere. Their commitment stemmed from a profound desire to forge a more equitable and prosperous future for their children and descendants. The villagers recognised the necessity of drastic action to safeguard their progeny's well-being.

In a unified front, the villagers of Duomduom came together and stood up for their beliefs. They paraded through the streets of Nhomlaau town with a fervour that could not be ignored. Their impassioned voices reverberated throughout the city as they made their demands known, leaving no doubt of their determination. Despite facing ridicule and opposition, the villagers remained resolute in their mission to safeguard their loved ones and their community.

A profound interdependence, a shared fate as tightly woven as the most sacred cloth, bound the impoverished citizens of Nhomlaau and the rural populace of Duomduom. Their fight for existence was a heroic, unrelenting struggle, not merely for their own immediate needs but for the enduring heritage they would bequeath to future generations. Ironically, this deep connection remained obscured by the stark divisions separating the two communities. The people of Duomduom, blinded by prejudice, mistakenly perceived the inhabitants of Nhomlaau solely as their oppressors.

Tensions between the Duomduom community and the Nhomlaau town's population escalated dramatically, solidifying a bitter stalemate. The initial dispute over the pilfered milk of Duomduom cattle became a mere spark, igniting a far greater conflagration. Whispers among the villagers evolved into a fervent claim that the conflict was a brutal struggle for territorial dominance and dwindling resources. The conflict, escalating with ferocious intensity, obliterated any semblance of rational discourse.

Unwavering in their positions, both factions remained locked in an implacable, unrelenting struggle.

The elders were split by the situation, sparking heated discussions. Some advocated for extreme measures, while others pursued nonviolent approaches. Those advocating drastic solutions believed that the only way to deal with the issue was to take extreme measures, while the other side argued that violence would only lead to further harm.

As the gap between these conflicting ideologies widened, so did the unease within the community. The scenario had created a profound schism among the elders, with each faction resolute in its pursuit of a resolution. It was clear that the elders were at a crossroads, and their decisions would have a profound impact on the community's future.

Flanking the seasoned warriors, who clamoured for immediate intervention, were the war-inexperienced masses of youth. Their eyes fixed on the captivating, almost primal authority of their leader, Gutgook Dhang Gutgook, the young men in the meeting shifted restlessly, their impatience barely masked by a veneer of composure.

Gutgook's formidable reputation was a prelude to his wartime leadership. Tales of his epic clashes resonated across the clans of Duomduom communities. He'd conquered fearsome creatures and vanquished opposing clans, his body a demonstration of his indomitable spirit, each scar a chronicle of unwavering bravery. But his eloquence, a weapon as sharp as any blade, proved equally devastating, captivating even the most cynical.

Gutgook conjured a compelling vision of a prosperous tomorrow, a future forged in the crucible of collective resolve and might. However, a disquieting undercurrent of suspicion churned beneath this veneer of promise. His ruthlessness and insatiable ambition became increasingly evident, fuelling a quiet rebellion. The embers of discontent were ignited.

Mesmerised by Gutgook's enigmatic allure, the young rebelled against the elders' stifling dominion. A thirst for liberation consumed them. Their audacious spirits propelled them into the forbidden wilds, craving experiences that transcended the village's confining embrace. Legends of primeval rites ignited their zealous pursuit. United by an insatiable curiosity, they felt ready to plunge into the unknown, confronting unforeseen companions and daunting obstacles. This was merely the genesis of their epic adventure.

The village elders were well aware of the danger Gutgook posed. His teachings were drawing the youth away from the traditional ways of the village, and they feared this would ultimately lead to a division within the community. They knew that if they didn't act fast, their village of Duomduom would be torn apart by conflict and chaos. The elders were determined to find a way to bring the youth back in line and preserve the unity of their village.

Recognising the futility of coercion, the sagacious elders understood that the allure of Gutgook's dogma couldn't be vanquished by brute force. A profound understanding dawned upon them: they must unearth the underlying reasons for the youth's fervent embrace of these teachings and offer a compelling counter-narrative. Thus, a council was convened, bringing together Gutgook, the impassioned young disciples, and the elders themselves. They aimed to forge a consensus, a resolution that would serve the collective good. By granting the youth a voice in this critical deliberation, the elders astutely hoped to cultivate a sense of ownership and respect, thereby fostering receptiveness to alternative viewpoints.

The elders' approach, however, was met with resistance from

Gutgook. He perceived their proposals as a blatant attempt at dominance. He cherished his singular viewpoint, a perspective honed by years of independent thought. His rebellious stance originated from a profound scepticism toward the elders' intentions, suspecting a calculated manoeuvre to manipulate the communal narrative. He felt marginalised, and his voice was stifled. This burgeoning discord threatened to shatter the community's fragile unity, leaving its trajectory ambiguous and heavily burdened by animosity. The future hung precariously in the balance.

A growing rift imperilled the village, jeopardising not just its communal harmony but its very survival. Immediate intervention was crucial, a remedy targeting the conflict's core. Daily, animosity festered, nourished by suspicion and terror. Indifference risked a devastating fracture. The village desperately needed a bold leader to champion reconciliation. Could a unifying ceremony, a bridge forged not of masonry but empathy, mend this profound fissure? The village's fate hung ominously in the balance.

Fuelled by resentment and anger toward the townspeople accused of milking cows in the bush, Gutgook had been plotting revenge. He believed that the townspeople had wronged their village in the past and that it was time for them to face the consequences of their actions. Despite the elders' efforts to maintain peace, the village was on the brink of chaos and division.

The older members, who had persevered through countless hardships, sought to maintain the hard-earned peace and stability. They contended that the wisest course of action would be to relocate the livestock far from the townspeople's reach.

However, the younger generation, who had grown up in relative calm, yearned to teach the town a lesson and were willing to resort to any means necessary to achieve it. Fuelled by simmering indignation at their elders' passive acceptance, a youthful rebellion began to brew. Their plan, a potent concoction of defiance, aimed to dismantle the town's suffocating inertia. This generation, ignited by enlightenment and a fervent desire for transformation, felt their pleas ignored, their voices lost in the complacent hum of the established order. The precise nature of their actions, however, remained cloaked in mystery. The looming confrontation threatened to fracture the town's façade of tranquillity, exposing the festering chasm of discord beneath.

The captivating leader Gutgook managed to manipulate the impressionable minds of the younger generation, exploiting their vulnerability and yearning for change. With skilful persuasion, he instilled in them a sense of moral superiority and convinced them that violence was the solution to their grievances. He wove a narrative of oppression and victimisation, positioning himself as the saviour who would guide them towards a brighter future. His rhetoric cast a potent enchantment, ensnaring the susceptible minds of the youth.

The younger generation was also deeply divided, caught between their allegiance to their community elders and their admiration for this enigmatic leader. As they became increasingly entangled in his web of deceit and manipulation, they lost sight of their principles and convictions, becoming mere pawns in his perilous quest for revenge.

The once tranquil community was in disarray, as the people were divided in their opinions. The elders, known for their wisdom and traditional beliefs, were determined to maintain the status quo. On the other hand, the youth, led by their charismatic leader, were eager to embrace change and usher in a new era of progress. The future of the Duomduom community hung in the balance as the two opposing sides battled for control.

The uncertainty was explicit as the community stood on the

brink of transformation. The community's fate rested on the choices that would be made in the days to come. Would the elders stay true to their beliefs or succumb to the allure of change? Would the youth be able to navigate the challenges that lay ahead and achieve their dreams? The answers would only be revealed with time as the villagers of Duomduom embarked on a journey towards an uncertain but promising future.

Chapter Three

A stalemate persisted in the ongoing feud between the older and younger generations, preventing a resolution of the conflict between Nhomlaau and Duomduom. Realising that a decision was necessary, Gutgook secretly summoned the youth for a meeting under the cover of night. The young ones responded positively, arriving as early as nine o'clock and standing in silence until Gutgook directed them to their designated seating areas, organised by clans.

As the meeting was about to commence, a low murmur of voices could be heard emanating from all corners of the gathering site. The young attendees were engaged in lively discussions, pondering over the possible agenda for the meeting. However, there was an unwavering trust in Gutgook as they eagerly awaited his instructions, their faces illuminated by the brilliant full moon, which also revealed their hidden meeting place and the vast wealth it held. Each member was equipped with sharpened spears and sturdy clubs, while a select few brandished swords acquired from a neighbouring town. Their collective demeanour displayed power and contemplation, profoundly impacting all.

Veteran commander Gutgook quelled the fervent whispers with a single gesture. Keenly assessing the eager throng, his eyes silently affirmed their collective resolve. A palpable tension thrummed; the young warriors, their newly crafted arms gleaming, fidgeted with barely contained zeal. Forged in the crucible of shared adversity and a yearning for liberation, their unity was an indomitable force. This critical juncture marked the beginning of their hazardous expedition, a courageous stride against the encroaching shadows. Though the road ahead remained shrouded in ambiguity, their unified spirit blazed with unwavering determination.

Deep as the earth itself, a tremor emanated from Gutgook's pronouncements, his words reverberating through the throng of gathered clans. His unflinching stare, a beacon of steadfast purpose, met every eye. Their spirits, forged in the crucible of ancestral suffering and an unshakeable devotion to their homeland, blazed with unwavering defiance. War loomed, a grim certainty. Heads cocked, they listened intently, bracing for the tumultuous days to come; their bravery, a fragile spark against the looming shadows of oblivion.

"My fellow brothers, you are all aware of the current situation between us and the elders," Gutgook began, his voice filled with frustration. "I have attempted to reason with them, but they persist in suggesting a passive approach. Some even go as far as proposing that we relocate our cattle camps far from the town to prevent the ones who milk our cows in the bush from accessing them. However, our other youth leaders and I do not view this as a feasible solution. How much longer must we remain idle?" He paused, scanning the faces of those around him, searching for someone to assign blame to.

The men around Gutgook shifted uncomfortably, each knowing that they were all in agreement with their leader's frustration. For years, they had been subjected to the constant theft of their cattle, and yet the elders refused to take any meaningful action. The young men, eager to protect their livelihood, were growing increasingly restless. Gutgook could sense their growing anger, and he knew that it was only a matter of time before they took matters into their own hands.

Gutgook's eyes fell upon the youngest member of their group, a boy barely reaching the age of manhood. The boy's name was Kuir, and he had only recently joined the cattle camp. Gutgook already knew that many of those gathered were too young to understand the gravity of the situation, but he also knew that they were not too young to fight for what was right. Kuir stood tall and proud, ready to do his part in ending the suffering of his people.

"I understand that some among you may be too young to engage in battle," Gutgook remarked, his gaze still fixed on Kuir. "However, for those of us who are of age and capable, we cannot simply stand by and watch our people suffer. The fact that even the youngest members, such as Kuir, have joined us here is a demonstration of their desire to end the suffering of innocent children. It is up to us to put an end to it."

"Allow me to update you, my comrades present at this gathering," Duaach Tong Duaach, also known as Fokosorot One, interrupted his superior. He was a respected leader among the youth of Duomduom. He had been Gutgook's right-hand man for many years and was well-known for his unwavering support and determination to achieve their common goals. As he addressed the gathering, his voice carried the weight of experience and authority. "I have known Gutgook for a long time, and I can assure you that he is a man of integrity and strong convictions. He will not rest until our community is free from the thieves who have been exploiting our cattle. We must stand behind him and offer our unwavering support, for it is only through unity and determination that we can achieve our liberation."

As Fokosorot One finished his speech, the youth erupted into cheers and applause. They were filled with renewed hope, ready to join the fight for their freedom. With their leaders by their side, they knew that nothing could stand in their way. The stage was set for a battle that would change the course of their lives forever.

Fokosorot One knew he had done what he needed to do to support his leader, Gutgook. His fiery rhetoric kindled a fervent blaze in the young community's liberation movement. He was assured because their jubilant shouts reverberated through the surrounding thicket, a resounding affirmation of their unyielding dedication. A profound burden of anticipation now settled upon the leaders, a responsibility they eagerly shouldered. This was their defining hour. Gutgook's solemn nod signified a shared understanding of the formidable challenge – a struggle to forge a future where hope transcended mere aspiration and blossomed into tangible existence. The path ahead promised to be fraught with hardship.

Gutgook thanked his companion for standing by him and then boldly declared, "I have no qualms in revealing the true culprit behind the missing milk from our cows. It is none other than Mr. Joseph Loi, the banker of Nhomlaau town. Who will be held responsible if we do not hold Mr. Loi accountable? Can we allow such a deceitful thief to flaunt his riches?"

The attendees exchanged bewildered glances. Their leader's words, unbelievable and shocking, hung in the air. The accusation levelled against Joseph Loi, the revered banker, cast a chilling shadow over the gathering. Gutgook's sombre pronouncements, a trivial infraction attributed to such a respected figure, created a jarring dissonance that shattered the villagers' composure. Suspicion, a poisonous vine, strangled the erstwhile tranquillity. The seemingly petty milk theft, now revealed as a mere manifestation of a far greater, more malevolent corruption, demanded immediate and rigorous investigation. The concealed reality, cloaked in enigma, yearned for exposure.

Deng Dumpiny Dit, also known as Forosorot Two, rose to his feet and swallowed hard, clearing his throat. He held the position of Secretary in Gutgook's administration. "I have always suspected that Mr. Loi was the mastermind behind the exploitation of our community," Deng started his speech. "I lacked the determination to investigate further. I am happy that our leader, Gutgook Dhang Gutgook, has discovered and revealed the truth. I will follow our leader's instructions to the letter. I urge all of us to unite and stand behind our leader."

The young were then stirred, their faces grave and determined. Rumblings of justice echoed through the crowd, and some urged immediate action against the perpetrator. They were eager to charge forward, their eyes ablaze with a fiery zeal. Others, however, were more hesitant, and they looked to Gutgook, their wise leader, for guidance and counsel.

Gutgook stood before the group of youthful individuals, his intense gaze capturing their attention. "My comrades," he began, "I implore patience. We must devise clear strategies to tackle this issue. Otherwise, we risk facing defeat in multiple ways."

Gutgook's pronouncements, steeped in the gravitas of a lifetime's battles, reverberated through the assembly. Almost every person in attendance agreed he underscored the absolute necessity of concerted effort, dismissing the fallacy of relying solely on individual prowess. Their looming predicament —a complex tapestry of perils —demanded a cohesive strategy. With a knowing glint in his eye, the young ones in the meeting believed that he hinted at insidious threats lurking beyond the obvious menace, unseen adversaries that demanded vigilance.

The weight of Gutgook's unspoken counsel hung heavy in the air, a palpable silence settling upon the assembled young warriors. A tremor of unease, a nascent fear, snaked through their ranks as the gravity of his warning fully registered. With chilling implications, he conveyed that their undertaking demanded far more than simple bravery. Astute planning, prescient judgment, and an adamantine will were equally indispensable.

"My counsel resonates, I perceive," Gutgook declared, his voice brimming with fervent conviction. His keen gaze, alight with lunar luminescence, interpreted the hushed expectancy as tacit agreement. "Meticulous planning, a cornerstone of triumph in conflict, demands our unwavering dedication. Let us ensure our readiness is absolute."

Gutgook was a master orator. As he continued to weave his persuasive arguments, the youths could feel the intensity of his words, the fear and danger that lurked around every corner. They were no longer just listening; they were living in the world that Gutgook was describing. His hands danced in the air, adding to the drama and suspense of his words. The full moon seemed to glow brighter as Gutgook's voice rose in urgency and the shadows cast by his hands deepened. The youths were mesmerised, hanging onto every word.

"Regarding preparations," Gutgook declared, his voice resonating with quiet strength, "my intent isn't to instil fear in you. I recognise your unwavering resolve to unshackle our villages from the avaricious merchants preying upon us, those who exploit our livestock in the wilds. They wield the law as a weapon, but our steadfast commitment is our shield."

Gutgook's gravelly voice, urgent and strained, depicted a menacing scene: heavily armed officers, their malevolent purpose unmistakable. He underscored the chasm separating their realities. The unsuspecting youths, blissfully unaware of the imminent peril, were at risk from a deadly threat. This innocence amplified the mounting tension, a substantial dread as the police presence inexorably advanced.

After Gutgook's stark warning, a suffocating silence descended again on the assembly, pierced only by the terrified, hushed murmurs of apprehension. The stark gravity of their predicament—the potential catastrophe looming—settled upon them like a crushing weight.

"In conclusion," Gutgook declared, "this undertaking requires minimal time. Your prompt readiness is paramount. I shall summon you immediately upon completing the necessary arrangements. My esteemed colleagues provide invaluable assistance here. Their competence inspires my unwavering confidence. I believe we will win, regardless of the dangers associated with our mission. We are men, and we must protect our people."

As Gutgook's speech came to an end, the youths were left in a state of shock and disbelief. They had never fully realised the gravity of their situation until now. The two worlds they had grown up in were vastly different, and they were living on the wrong side of the cloud of ignorance. Gutgook's repeated mention of danger had opened their eyes to the harsh reality of their existence, and they were now faced with a difficult decision. Would they continue living in fear and ignorance, or would they rise and fight for their rights and a better future?

This revelation of danger associated with the mission the youths were embarking on—a concealed truth of staggering proportions—held the potential for unparalleled dominion alongside horrific, unforeseen perils. Their established convictions shattered beneath the weight of this profound discovery. A potent cocktail of apprehension and exhilaration seized the youths as they wrestled with its ramifications. They stood on the precipice of a transformative journey into the uncharted. What formidable obstacles would they confront?

After a brief period of silence, Fokosorot Two rose from his seat and declared, "Our esteemed leader, Gutgook, is diligently working towards our success. He has tirelessly gathered evidence and prepared to expose the rampant corruption plaguing our people. Now, he proposes a course of action. The tactical team always exercises caution. Let us heed his words. He has spent more time in town than Fokosorot One and I and has been well-informed."

Gutgook was watching the youth keenly as Fokosorot Two spoke. The group before him were the young, eager minds of the next generation, and he knew that they were the ones who would bring actual change to their world. He could see in their eyes that they were taking in every word, their faces reflecting the same determination that burned within him. The cloud of ignorance that had shrouded their village was slowly being lifted, and with it, the people were beginning to see the truth. No longer would they allow themselves to be taken advantage of, nor would they ignore the rampant corruption.

"Remember, friends, that we are not discouraging you from your determination to act against the banker who steals milk from our cows," Gutgook resumed his speech. His words were like a beacon of hope, guiding the youth towards a better future. As the moon rose higher in the sky, Gutgook continued to speak, his voice strong and unwavering. "I just want us to approach the issues tactically. It will not take us too long before we put everything right."

As each moment passed, the audience of Gutgook became increasingly convinced that they possessed the power to effect change. They were determined to put an end to the harmful actions of a select few individuals, which had long been concealed by ignorance. Together, they would unite against the injustices that had plagued their village of Duomduom for too long. However, they agreed that their course of action must be carefully orchestrated to avoid any undesirable outcomes.

Fokosorot One proposed collecting additional evidence to substantiate Mr. Loi's accusations of stealing milk from Duomduom's cows. Gutgook concurred with this suggestion but suggested that the community's youth take the lead in the investigation, while the older members refrain from involvement. According to him, this approach would ensure a thorough and unbiased inquiry.

Other members of the youth leadership supported the recommendation to provide additional evidence. However, Fokosorot One's proposition elicited a mixed response from the group. Some were in favour, believing that involving only the younger generation in the investigation would result in a more thorough and impartial outcome. Others were hesitant and concerned that the exclusive youth team's involvement in such a sensitive matter could cause community tensions.

Despite the disagreements and uncertainties, the group finally decided to proceed with Fokosorot One's suggestion. The exclusive team of youth members eagerly took on the task, determined to uncover the truth and bring justice to Duomduom's communities. This decision marked a pivotal point in the community's dynamics, as it challenged the traditional roles and hierarchy of the elders. It also showed the younger generation's willingness to take responsibility and make a positive change in their community.

Gutgook rose and officially adjourned the assembly after the conclusive articulation of action items. He urged the young attendees to disperse discreetly, avoiding any commotion within the village. His instructions were accurately followed. The participants departed in small, unassuming clusters. Meanwhile, the specially appointed committee, charged with thoroughly examining milk production in Nhomlaau, remained, methodically plotting their investigative strategy before departing.

The inquiry commenced the following morning. The investigative team's probing questions regarding market transactions yielded frustratingly inconclusive results. The inherent impenetrability of the supply chain—with the same individuals both acquiring and dispensing the milk—prevented the extraction of credible data. Fearful of jeopardising the fragile trust with the Duomduom villagers, already deeply distrustful of the milk's origin, the team's sources remained stubbornly silent about their suppliers.

After three days, Gutgook gathered a group of young leaders and disclosed that the evidence regarding the banker's involvement was still inconclusive. Nonetheless, he asserted that Mr. Loi, the banker residing in Nhomlaau town, was the true culprit behind the theft of milk from Duomduom's cows. Some of the other youth leaders supported Gutgook's assertion, concurring that the town's banker was the underlying cause of their persistent struggles. They were convinced that this man was the mastermind orchestrating their exploitation, representing the town's unbridled greed and corruption.

Duomduom's youthful vanguard ignited a coalition fuelled by a burning resentment towards the banker's exploitative schemes. Their audacious strategy unfolded in clandestine operations.

To circumvent the interference of the entrenched gerontocracy, each leader covertly rallied their respective kindred, holding furtive gatherings shrouded in secrecy. The young generation's unwavering commitment foreshadowed a formidable confrontation against the corruptible establishment. The appointed day arrived—a synchronised uprising. Clans convened at disparate locations, simultaneously ensuring the elders remained oblivious to the coordinated defiance brewing beneath their noses.

The appointed day dawned without incident. The young people maintained a façade of normalcy. However, nightfall unleashed a clandestine movement. They dispersed, shadows gliding to separate clan gathering places. Secret councils convened under the cloak of darkness; hushed conversations replaced any open declarations of defiance. Each budding rebel meticulously selected trusted allies.

These furtive gatherings fuelled a nascent rebellion, steadily undermining the elders' authority with each whispered oath of opposition. The banker's greed, a cruel twist of fate, had unwittingly forged a powerful alliance, ready to shatter his dominion. Their plan was fraught with danger, but their unwavering unity proved to be their most potent weapon.

With hearts thumping, the youth leaders of different clans commenced their sectional meetings. A fervent conviction in a gleaming future propelled their actions. Their painstaking facilitation ensured that each voice was heard, fostering a sense of collective empowerment. This unified endeavour exponentially magnified their influence. The atmosphere vibrated with a tangible sense of urgency and determination. A revolutionary tide was poised to peak. Once shrouded in doubt, the future now felt remarkably attainable.

The spirits of the participants were united like constellations in the heavens. Although they came from different families and age backgrounds, they were all bound by a common cause. Their hearts beat as one, their voices raised in unison, and their minds focused on the task at hand. They were warriors in the making, ready to fight for what they believed in, and nothing could stand in their way. Their collective goal was clear: to bring down the wealthy magnate.

A violent uprising appeared to erupt amongst Duomduom's young people. Whispers of rebellion, escalating into a full-blown insurgency, unexpectedly forged alliances among those united by shared grievances. Weeks of seething resentment and disillusionment, stemming from the perceived exploitation of their livestock by the alleged Nhomlaau banker's alleged cronies, fuelled their strategy's meticulous crafting. Their objective was to dismantle the banker's absolute power.

That night in Duomduom, a shared aspiration eclipsed all else among the clans' young men. Their secret pact, born under the cloak of darkness, promised exhilaration and peril in equal measure. A compelling cocktail of reckless courage and a profound yearning for transformation propelled them toward their audacious undertaking. The dire ramifications hung heavy in the air, yet their determination remained unyielding. The gravity of their choice bore down upon them, but the siren song of triumph spurred them onward, their pulses thrumming with a potent blend of trepidation and exhilaration. Their journey had merely commenced.

An hour following the meeting, youth leaders and secretaries from various Duomduom clans commenced arriving at Gutgook's residence. Each delivered their meticulously crafted decisions with terse efficiency, departing immediately afterwards. This solemn procession continued for two hours, a silent demonstration of the weight of their pronouncements. Finally, Gutgook collated the documents, their significance unmistakable, before withdrawing to his chambers, the gravity of the morrow's deliberations heavy upon him.

The following dawn, Gutgook, having digested the disparate pronouncements from the various tribal factions, summoned his most trusted lieutenants. His powerful voice, a resonant instrument of command, articulated each clan's decision. This proclamation ignited a fierce exchange, a crucible of competing viewpoints hammered out in the white heat of argument. Unwavering in their commitment, Gutgook and his loyal young commanders embraced the resolutions, their determination unyielding despite the looming threat of the banker's impending financial entanglement. They stood ready for conflict, their courage as indomitable as a mother bear defending her offspring from a relentless predator.

In the resolutions that Gutgook and his other senior youth leaders discussed and approved, unanimous fury seemed to erupt at every clan meeting. They all agreed that a greedy banker's crimes, even his attempts at cheating death, could not escape retribution. A fierce, collective desire for justice seemed to burn bright in each document, resolute in its intensity. The youths in their meetings decided to remain unyielding, their resolve unshakeable until the scales of justice were balanced. Each meeting's resolution echoed the others, stating that the corrupt magnate's wickedness would inevitably bring consequences. A tangible thirst for vengeance, a raging inferno threatening to consume all, hung heavy in the air.

Having consolidated the diverse resolutions of Duomduom village's clans into a single, powerful proclamation, Gutgook dispatched his most trusted youth leaders. These leaders, including Fokosorot One, fanned out across the village. Their mission was to ignite the hearts of the youth. They delivered a compelling message that their struggle for justice would redress past wrongs and forge a radiant future for all. The young people's bravery and unwavering determination, it was proclaimed, would ignite a transformative movement, relentlessly pursuing equity and fairness within their community.

As time passed, Gutgook's hold over the youth grew more potent and more insidious. He knew exactly how to tap into their sentiments and anxieties, manipulating them like puppets on a string. They were convinced that Joseph Loi and his workers were a threat to their way of life and that Gutgook was the only one who could protect them. He played on their fears and insecurities, gradually becoming their untouchable leader and the one they looked to for guidance. It was a tale of two worlds - one controlled by Gutgook's deceit and another that was struggling to resist his influence.

Gutgook delighted in his dominion, a leader enthroned by the young's unwavering devotion. Their blind faith, a fierce and absolute loyalty, was a weapon he wielded with chilling precision. He demanded, and they obeyed without question, their actions reflecting the depths of their subservience, regardless of peril. His carefully orchestrated machinations relentlessly pursued a singular objective: the annihilation of Joseph Loi and his associates, thereby asserting his tyrannical reign over the village.

Five days later, Gutgook called for another gathering of the young people at the exact location where they had first met. This was also done under the cover of darkness, just as the first meeting in which he introduced the youth to his ideas. He shared his plan for taking down the banker. He revealed his plot to strike at Joseph Loi and his financial institution. Gutgook said this was retribution for the wealthy banker's alleged exploitation of the villagers' resources. In his distorted version of events, Joseph was portrayed as a malicious figure, exploiting the villagers' innocence and vulnerability for his selfish gain.

Fuelled by a venomous loathing for Joseph, Gutgook concocted a scheme of brutal retribution. His goal was to shatter the bedrock of Nhomlaau's affluence, the very edifice Joseph had painstakingly constructed. Driven by pitiless mischievousness, he sought the utter annihilation of Joseph and his financial dominion, indifferent to the catastrophic consequences for the innocent villagers. In Gutgook's twisted morality, this act of devastation was the sole means of rectifying the profound imbalance he perceived in his ravaged existence.

Despite Gutgook's belief that he was the hero and Joseph the villain, his actions would have significant repercussions for both of them and the entire village. He failed to foresee the far-reaching consequences of his scheme, which would ultimately unravel the carefully constructed world he knew. Gutgook's plan became more evident as the nights and days progressed, and the stakes grew higher.

Unwittingly, the youths embarked on their expedition, utterly unaware of the perilous snare that awaited them. Gutgook's assertions, devoid of substantiation, served only to ensnare them further. Masterfully manipulated by his insidious guile, these innocent souls found themselves entangled in a deadly labyrinth. This alluring yet treacherous journey held the terrifying potential to alter the fate of both realms irrevocably.

The youths, however, were not to be blamed for being so easily deceived by Gutgook. They were young and naive, and their hearts were filled with a burning desire for justice. Gutgook's rhetoric blinded them, along with some elders who were supposed to be wise and experienced. They failed to realise that Gutgook's true intentions were far from noble.

Gutgook's deceptive cloud of confusion enveloped his followers like a thick fog. They were unable to see the harsh reality through it. It was only when the tragic consequences of their misguided decisions became undeniable did they finally realise the true extent of his cunning schemes and the devastating destruction they had caused.

Chapter Four

Following rapid and enthusiastic youth assemblies, Gutgook, the self-proclaimed paramount leader of Duomduom village's young people, summoned his most trusted senior youth leaders, including Fokosorot One and Fokosorot Two. They aimed to formulate an unsympathetic strategy for assaulting the banker and his cronies in Nhomlaau. Gutgook's fiery rhetoric was escalating into cold-blooded resolve, poised to exact savage retribution upon the banker he blamed for the systematic pilfering of Duomduom's dairy herds.

From his central dwelling, a stark edifice dominating the assembly, Gutgook surveyed his subordinates. His eyes, keen as hooks, fixed on each face, conveying the gravity of the situation. A hawk's severe appearance, etched into his features, underscored the pressing need for immediate action. He spat forcefully, a projectile aimed at the mud wall, then nonchalantly smeared the spittle away. His resonant voice, a deep rumble, filled the chamber. "My associates," he boomed, "speediness is essential. Delay is an unforgivable transgression."

Gutgook's combustible opening statement kindled a furious blaze of determination in the assembled senior youth leaders. Their suppressed rage erupted, a volcanic torrent fuelled by the banker's greediness, a plague that had infected them all. His immediate call for speedy action struck a thoughtful chord, promising swift and merciless retribution for the villagers' endured hardships. A long-extinguished ember of hope rekindled, casting off the suffocating darkness. However, chilling anxiety persisted. Some of the leaders murmured of the banker's formidable might, their influence a thread strangling the very life from the land far beyond the city's fortifications. The road to justice would be fraught with peril.

After some seconds of silence, a thoughtful debate over the optimal strategy erupted. Some leaders advocated a swift, merciless seizure, while others proposed a more furtive penetration. The formidable security surrounding the banker's house cast a long shadow over their discussions. Plans to sever communications and establish secure escape pathways were painstakingly detailed, leaving the final, decisive attack plan still under intense consideration.

After gazing at the leaders before him for a while, Gutgook's chest constricted with empathy. The inexperienced senior youth leaders' apprehension mirrored his agonising self-doubt of yesteryear. A profound responsibility settled upon him. He perceived their latent power, a fragile spark threatened by the winds of adversity, demanding his steadfast guidance. The crushing burden of their destiny bore down on them. He steeled their resolve, foreseeing trials that would relentlessly test their determination, a crucible that would forge their indomitable spirits.

"Dear comrades," Gutgook addressed the young leaders of his administration with confidence. "I am seeing the pieces falling into place. Our plans to address Mr. Loi's concerns are progressing smoothly. Like you, I am determined to guide our people out of the grips of exploitation that has plagued them for weeks. My methods may be unconventional, but I have a clear vision in mind—one where my people are no longer bound by ignorance and poverty. This vision is familiar to all of you. Let us put our minds together and brainstorm ways to make it a reality. Our first step will be to stop the banker and his accomplice from stealing from us."

Initially, Gutgook's severe countenance instilled fear in them. Yet, as he turned his attention to their worries, his expression mellowed, revealing a depth of understanding born from shared adversity. His counsel, forged in the crucible of countless struggles, flowed from a wellspring of hard-earned wisdom. Beneath his imposing physique resided a compassionate soul, his empathy a persuasive consolation. Initially overwhelmed by his formidable presence, the young people gradually came to perceive the genuine warmth beneath the intimidating façade. Their admiration, consequently, deepened into profound respect.

Swiftly, Gutgook assumed the mantle of leadership, shouldering the immense burden of his people's hopes. He grasped the profound significance of his choices and the latent capabilities and bright prospects blooming within each individual. His duty, a sacred trust, was to shepherd them toward this radiant future, to vanquish their anxieties and doubts, mirroring the guidance he had received at his very young age.

"I think the banker will have a rude awakening when we show him how much we value our community and its assets," Gutgook explained. "We will teach him a lesson that will earn us the respect we deserve. I guarantee you this lesson will not be forgotten easily."

Gutgook's voice reverberated with the weight of countless hardships endured for the benefit of others. "My life," he declared, "has been a tapestry woven with threads of selflessness." He paused, letting the gravity of his words sink in. "Each of you possesses a unique capacity for compassion, a distinct path toward alleviating suffering. But if we, as a collective body of young capable people, cannot summon the courage to relinquish our comfort for the sake of those innocent children, now starved and vulnerable, then who will?"

The rhetorical question that Gutgook asked as he ended the statement carried the gravity of imminent retribution against the banker and his associates in Nhomlaau town. Knowing his decisive nature, Gutgook's colleagues in the meeting anticipated swift action on his vow to redress the banker's transgressions. They envisioned a pivotal confrontation, a transformative experience intended to instil profound respect for their community and its precious resources.

"We stand resolute," Gutgook declared, his voice ringing with conviction, "united in our unwavering belief that the lives of our offspring rest solely upon our shoulders. We seek no handouts, no charity. Our livestock, honestly earned and ethically raised, are our sustenance. The audacious theft of their milk by unscrupulous businesspeople in the town of Nhomlaau is an intolerable transgression. We are bound by duty, by the sacred trust of parenthood, to ensure such predatory actions are never repeated."

Gutgook's unwavering belief, born from the crucible of personal hardship, profoundly moved his young colleagues. His guidance was more than mere direction; it was a profound understanding that illuminated their struggles, offering a deeper insight into their challenges. This shared moment of insight revealed a compassionate core to his leadership, showcasing the steadfast dedication of a protector fiercely devoted to the growth of his community.

Driven by a thirst for knowledge yet haunted by the ominous shadow of a potential assault on Nhomlaau, the young leaders in the meeting yearned for clarity. Though their village origins were diverse, a shared aspiration united them: a community cleansed of the insidious theft of milk. Gutgook, their guiding light and surrogate father, had forged this unlikely alliance. He possessed an intuitive grasp of their hardships, recognising their desperate need for sage counsel to traverse the treacherous terrain of their existence.

"All that we have agreed on in this meeting," Gutgook said, "should be implemented as soon as we leave this compound. Time is of the essence, and we must not waste it. Victory is within our reach. Each minute lost could mean a lost battle."

The assembled senior youth leaders felt a profound sense of urgency. Their silent nods to Gutgook's words emphasised the imperative for swift intervention. The daunting challenge before them was apparent. Yet, their unyielding, enthusiastic hope ignited fierce determination. Gutgook's pronouncements, an encouragement in the encroaching darkness, charted a course toward a flourishing Duomduom. His stirring call to action, a resonant battle cry, deeply resonated, solidifying their passionate commitment to wresting control of their dairy resources from the avaricious hands of those exploiting their community's rightful heritage.

"The most crucial advice I can impart to you," Gutgook cautioned, "is to guard our secret closely. The days of preparation we have ahead of us may be put at risk if our plans are revealed. Instruct the younger members of your clans to exercise utmost caution in what they divulge, even to their parents. We must demonstrate maturity in this matter, as it is in our best interest. When any of you visit Nhomlaau, remember that you will be perceived as outsiders. They may appear curious about your activities in the village, but do not confide in them."

A deep, crimson light blazed, casting incongruous, elongated shadows that whirled with a floating tenacity. Terror, thick and suffocating, forged an unbreakable link between them. Gutgook's stratagem relied on swiftness and stealth. Their mutual danger sharpened their resolve into a razor's edge. Each inhale was a desperate plea for deliverance. Their unkempt garments and grime-caked hands provided a cloak of invisibility, merging them seamlessly with the murk of Duomduom's underworld as they dispersed. The undertaking was fraught with mortal danger; the consequences of failure were catastrophic.

Leaving Gutgook's dwelling, the senior youth leaders silently returned to their quarters. The drab hues of their environment served as a grim, persistent testament to the pervasive threat encircling Duomduom. A palpable sense of urgency gripped the group. They were bound by an unwavering commitment to Gutgook's edicts, understanding that absolute obedience was the only shield against the perils of this unfamiliar reality.

Gutgook's injunction was absolute. Their departure must be shrouded in the most profound secrecy. The plan's success hinged on swift, silent action, a point underscored by the solemn, repeated nods of the youth leaders. They fully grasped the perilous nature of their undertaking. Each clan head bore the weighty responsibility of equipping their young warriors—providing them with ample sustenance, vital survival tools, and the implements of their rigorous training. The jungle's inherent perils demanded meticulous preparation. Their foray into the heart of Nhomlaau's territory, Gutgook stressed, depended entirely on the element of surprise and the lethal proficiency cultivated during their covert jungle exercises. The fate of the operation, he had declared grimly, rested solely on their capable shoulders.

Under the cloak of night, hardened youth leaders subtly

disseminated the crucial Gutgook directives among their fellow clan members. Younger members not yet initiated into adulthood in every clan—such as Kuir—and young initiates deemed insufficiently mature were intentionally excluded from this concealed information. Only those who had formally achieved adulthood, per ancient tribal rites, and were regarded as sufficiently mature received the solemn command to penetrate the forbidding depths of the jungle for their rigorous war training.

Two days later, all the able-bodied youth gathered at a single point and moved toward a designated location in the jungle. Most of them were timid and hesitant, as they were not accustomed to venturing beyond the safe confines of their village. But as they followed Gutgook deeper into the jungle, they began to open up. They started asking many questions about the mission.

Gutgook, ever cautious, withheld the whole, brutal reality. The truth, he sensed, would overwhelm these young minds. He simply informed them of his intent to forge them into instruments ready for the imminent assault on Nhomlaau. With the precision of a master sculptor, he meticulously shaped their understanding, each carefully chosen word a brushstroke on the canvas of their minds. He recognised their eagerness, absorbent nature, and capacity to soak in every lesson. His unwavering confidence, a blazing star, illuminated their path toward triumph over Nhomlaau.

As they walked and talked, Gutgook couldn't help but reminisce about his journey. His past relentlessly clawed at him, each footfall a mournful testament to his suffering. He had witnessed atrocities beyond comprehension, a stark juxtaposition to the carefree mirth of the lads. The spectres of his experiences relentlessly pursued him, solidifying his solemn oath to safeguard these youths, to interpose a bulwark against the savagery he knew so intimately. He would be their mentor, their unwavering guardian. The journey promised to be arduous; the world was a pitiless courtesan. But within his heart, an unyielding resolve ignited a fervent commitment to their well-being, a beacon burning brightly against the encroaching darkness.

After a long and exhausting journey through the dense jungle, they finally arrived at a clearing. In the far distance, the towering buildings of Nhomlaau town stood in stark contrast to the humble dwellings of their village. The youth's eyes widened with a mix of wonder and trepidation, and Gutgook understood that their true journey was about to begin. This was the exact place where they would undergo rigorous training, constantly reminded by the urban landscape that their mission to attack the banker's residence was imminent.

A tight circle of colleagues, eyes fixed on Gutgook, awaited the final arrival. He surveyed the assembled group, then, with a decisive cough, began. "Welcome, my friends, to this secluded sanctuary of skill. Nearby, the brook murmurs—its icy waters a constant refreshment against the thirst of exertion. Though distant towers pierce the horizon, this haven remains undisturbed —a refuge untouched by the city's bustle. I underwent a similar rigorous apprenticeship here years past—hence my intimate familiarity with this place."

When Gutgook first left his home and got the war training at the same training ground, he was like the people he now watched. He was young and naive, believing that the world was full of good. As the years passed, he came to see the truth: wars, hatred, and destruction. He quickly learned that he needed to conceal his true intentions and keep a low profile to survive.

Following the initial greetings, Gutgook strategically assigned the clans to their designated training zones. He meticulously subdivided each clan into ten-man units, appointing one of them as the leader. From his central command post, erected at the heart of the encampment, Gutgook oversaw the groups with iron discipline. His directives were executed with unwavering precision.

With the sun's descent, a hush fell over the clans as they diligently prepared their evening meal. A low hum of anticipation, a vibrant tapestry woven from whispered conversations, hinted at the momentous events to come. Then, at the stroke of midnight, a profound stillness fell over the training grounds, a palpable sense of expectancy hanging heavy in the air.

Training commenced the following day. Gutgook, the sole instructor, observed the young trainees' arduous struggle to meet the brutal demands of the training exercises. He perceived their peril acutely. Failure to master these skills swiftly would condemn them to the same grim destiny as countless predecessors. He understood, with a chilling certainty, the impossibility of saving every single one. This harsh reality, a bitter lesson etched into his very being, was the price of survival. As he continued his rigorous tutelage, he fervently hoped they would learn from his past failures and eventually break free from the suffocating veil of apathy.

Gutgook stressed the importance of time, knowing that it was a fleeting enemy. He was determined to impart his knowledge before it was too late. Despite initial hesitation, the youth were eager to listen. They knew that the very existence of their community depended on them, and their survival was at risk if they remained ignorant. With rapt attention, Gutgook emphasised the importance of keeping secrets. He knew that this was their only hope against the perils of ignorance.

Gutgook's profound wisdom inspired the young people, who realised that their survival in this transformed world depended on their ability to adapt and learn. His powerful message resonated with them, igniting a strong sense of commitment to his teachings. The impact of his words was visible in their actions as they embraced his tutelage with unwavering determination. His influence continued to guide them on their journey towards growth and evolution as young warriors of Duomduom communities.

The rigorous teachings, embraced with passionate devotion, became the foundation for the youths' survival. They understood these instructions as a transformative legacy, a precious boon for which their hearts overflowed with immeasurable thankfulness. Captivated, their gazes remained locked upon Gutgook. His weathered features, engraved with the trials of life, held them engrossed as he unveiled a world previously relegated to myth. His voice, gaining power with each utterance, resonated with youthful vigour, weaving them into the tapestry of his narrative. The surrounding lush vegetation served as a poignant reminder of a bygone era, a cherished past now receding into the hazy mists of memory.

Immersed in Gutgook's vivid recounting of his training, the adolescents felt their identities intertwine with his narrative, their understanding blossoming with each revelation. The vibrant foliage surrounding them pulsed with life, mirroring the dynamism of Gutgook's extravaganza. With each passing night, the young trainees underwent a profound transformation, one that was indelibly marked by Gutgook's powerful story.

With boundless patience and profound wisdom, Gutgook, a mentor of exceptional calibre, unveiled the wilderness's enigmatic secrets to the young trainees. Jungle treks became immersive lessons, with each vibrant avian marvel meticulously identified and its symbolic meaning deeply explored. Astonishment radiated from the youths; their eyes, alight with fervent curiosity, drank in the forest's breathtaking splendour. From the murmuring canopy's hushed whispers to the ethereal luminescence dappling the forest floor, the awe-inspiring beauty held them captive.

With each lesson, Gutgook showed the youths the interconnectedness of all living things and how humans were just one small part of a larger ecosystem. He taught them to respect and care for the environment, knowing that everything was connected in a delicate balance. As they continued their training, the youth began to see the world in a different light. They no longer saw nature as just a backdrop or something to be conquered, but as a living and breathing entity.

The youth learned that every action they took, no matter how small, could have an impact on the world around them. Gutgook showed them how to listen to the whispers of the forest, to understand the language of the animals, and to appreciate the world's beauty. And as their understanding grew, so did their love and respect for the wild. The cattle they treasured were animals like those found in the wild. They realised that true wisdom came not from conquering or controlling but from observing and understanding.

Gutgook smiled as he watched the youth's appreciation for the natural world blossom before his very eyes. As the day drew to a close and they returned to their camp for the night, Gutgook knew this was just the beginning of the youth's journey. He had seen the spark of understanding and appreciation within them, and he knew that with time and guidance, they would become skilled and respectful members of their tribe. For Gutgook, it was a privilege to pass on the knowledge and wisdom of their people to the younger generation, and he looked forward to witnessing the youth's growth and development in the days to come.

Under a shroud of rigorous training steeped in absolute confidentiality, their mission hung precariously. Gutgook, their unwavering leader, grimly emphasised that assassinating the banker was their sole lifeline in this unforgiving new reality. Exposure meant utter annihilation, a complete expulsion from a society that already viewed them as pariahs. These displaced souls, exiles from a forgotten world, acutely felt the sting of prejudice and alienation. Their survival demanded absolute camouflage. Their true purpose was veiled in impenetrable secrecy. With relentless dedication, they honed their strategy, each component meticulously refined until unshakeable conviction fuelled their impending action. Failure was unthinkable; success, their only salvation, demanded every ounce of their resolve.

Although the training was gruelling, it was essential for the young people's survival in the unforgiving environment surrounding Nhomlaau. Gutgook understood the stark reality: defeat meant banishment to the merciless jungle, a potential death sentence that could last a year. Forging mutual trust and a collaborative spirit became paramount despite their internal conflicts. Their strategy was finalised, a desperate gamble against overwhelming odds.

A substantial fear, a silent menace, gripped Nhomlaau, clinging to its very foundations. The town's revered banker, Mr. Loi, remained oblivious to the gathering darkness, unaware of its approach. Conversely, the young people of Duomduom village, acutely sensing the impending devastation, embraced Gutgook's wise advice with unwavering dedication. Their spirits were ignited by a fierce resolve to safeguard their dairy herds and precious milk from the plunderers lurking within Nhomlaau's shadowed passageways.

Meanwhile, in Duomduom village, the youth had deserted into the jungle for their ongoing training, leaving the older members to carry on with their daily lives, unaware of the impending danger. The younger generation couldn't help but notice the older members' ignorance and prayed that they would be spared from the impending chaos.

Unbeknownst to the impetuous young men of Duomduom, the elders harboured deep anxieties. These anxieties, however, were not for their safety. Seasoned veterans of countless brutal conflicts, the elders possessed an unshakeable fortitude born of harrowing experiences. War held no terrors for them. Their apprehension resided solely in the untested hearts of their successors. Except for the battle-hardened Gutgook, the youth, fuelled by tales of glorious combat, yearned to test their courage. Their naive enthusiasm was a chilling portent to the elders' worried gaze.

When the community chiefs and esteemed elders learned that the young ones were receiving training in the wilderness, they were compelled to visit. When they arrived at the designated area, Gutgook sounded the whistle, and the youth swiftly gathered on the field for a parade. They positioned themselves on one side, while the community leaders and elders stood on the other.

The generational divide was evident in the contrasting emotions of the youth and the elders. While the youth were filled with passion and energy, the elders were burdened with the weight of experience. The two worlds of the young and old collided as they stood side by side, preparing for the unknown.

After a brief moment of silence, the Executive Chief of Duomduom strode to the front and coughed to capture the audience's attention. "My dear ones," he addressed them, "you have gathered here, and it is evident that we were not informed of this. Gutgook, please tell us, what brings you to this place?"

Gutgook strode to the front, ensuring that all eyes were on him. He then cleared his throat and glanced around, spitting into the air. "My esteemed fathers," he began, "I am delighted by your presence. We, your children, are under your watchful care, and it is only natural for you to be concerned for us. Rest assured, we are all safe and sound.

"Regarding your inquiry, I am unable to disclose our purpose here. However, our actions were simply an exercise, harmless to all. Would you not agree?"

The Executive Chief replied, "I respectfully disagree. Let us speak honestly. You have expressed dissatisfaction with individuals whom you have accused of unlawfully extracting milk from our cattle and selling it in Nhomlaau town. As elders, we have discussed this matter with you, emphasising the importance of handling it peacefully. Yet, you persist in your disagreement. It appears to us that you are preparing for conflict."

"Conflict with who?" asked Gutgook without hesitation.

"Conflict with townspeople," replied the Executive Chief.

"Uncle," Gutgook replied, "that's just your perspective. We are simply engaging in physical activity here. Your perception of our exercise may hold as we prepare for the aftermath of your peaceful resolution endeavours. I encourage you to proceed with your plans to resolve the issue. Let us be and return to us once the issue has been resolved."

It was a classic tale of youthful rebellion and seasoned wisdom, with each side convinced of its righteousness. The young saw their elders as outdated and incapable of understanding the struggles of the modern world, while the elders viewed the youth as impulsive and reckless. The two worlds seemed to be on a collision course, with no one willing to step back and find a middle ground.

As the debate raged on between Gutgook and the Executive Chief, it became clear that this was not just a simple disagreement between generations. It was a battle for the soul of Duomduom village, with each side fighting for what they believed was best for their community. It reflected a larger conflict that divided not just generations but entire communities.

Whispers and hushed conversations revealed growing

suspicions, while worried expressions gave away the unease.

Noticing the shift in the expressions of the Executive Chief and some elders, Gutgook addressed them, "My Chief, I sense anger in you, but I assure you, I have no ill intentions toward our community. I am still your son, and your worries are mine as well. I urge you to take a moment to contemplate this matter."

The Executive Chief glanced at his team for a moment before directing his attention to Gutgook again. With a calm demeanour, he assured him, "My dear son, I harbour no anger towards you. However, we will keep a watchful eye on your actions."

Gutgook nodded in agreement.

The Executive Chief then turned, made his way through the council of elders, and began his journey back to the village. His entire team, who had accompanied him from the village, followed behind, leaving the youth behind in the field. As they trekked through the dense jungle, they engaged in conversation about the potential outcomes of the youth's training until they finally reached the village once more.

The youth gathered around Gutgook, who revealed that the elders were displeased. The others nodded in agreement, having perceived the underlying frustration in their elders' expressions. The once-tranquil village was now disturbed, and the youth were on edge, their eyes darting around anxiously. The intensity of the situation was akin to a raging storm, leaving them on high alert. However, Gutgook told the youth that the mission should proceed. He argued that giving up would be more dangerous than executing the plan.

Rumours quickly spread throughout the village and Nhomlaau town, igniting the already tense atmosphere. Whispers of sinister forces and internal betrayal only added to the townspeople's fear and uncertainty. Caught between their desire for the truth and their fear of the unknown, it was clear that something was amiss. As the days passed, the divide between their familiar reality and the looming danger became more apparent, thickening the tension in the town.

Despite the impending danger, Joseph Loi, the town's banker, remained unfazed. He carried himself with confidence and composure, continuing his daily activities without knowledge of the impending chaos. His demeanour baffled the townspeople, who were frantically preparing for the worst. Some whispered that Mr. Loi must have some inside information, while others praised his bravery in the face of uncertainty.

Mr. Loi's intransigence was a granite wall. The impending doom was tangible to the townsfolk, yet he, a lifelong cynic, dismissed their anxieties as unwarranted hysteria. He clung to a naive faith in the eventual restoration of normalcy. But the town's youth and the constabulary, acutely aware of the imminent peril, were resolute in their efforts to save their community. They were determined to shatter Mr. Loi's complacent delusion, to pierce the veil of his wilful blindness before it was too late.

The ominous signs were undeniable. A sense of impending catastrophe hung heavy in the air. The urgency of the situation propelled the young and the police into swift action. They began vigilant patrols around the bank and the town's perimeter. However, Mr. Loi remained steadfast in his denial, paralysed by fear-induced blindness. His recalcitrance created a chasm in the city, fracturing its unity. Some people remained loyal to his misguided conviction, while others rallied to the police's cause, their resolve hardened by the escalating threat.

Chapter Five

As the looming threat drew closer, Mr. Loi's stoic facade began to crack. His wife and children noticed the bags under his eyes and his constant fidgeting, signs of his growing anxiety. Yet, he remained determined to keep up appearances for the sake of his family and the town. No one knew that behind closed doors, he was pouring over financial records, trying to find a way to protect his family and his assets from potential attackers.

The unspoken terror for Mr. Loi's family's well-being consumed him, a silent anguish demonstrable to those who loved him. Their quiet support was a solace to his tormented spirit, a demonstration of their shared apprehension. He sought refuge in careful preparation, a frantic bid to wrestle back some measure of control from the encroaching darkness. Maintaining a façade of serenity, he secretly braced for catastrophe, desperately clinging to a flicker of hope against the mounting threat. Each tick of the clock amplified the impending peril.

Rumours of a brutal, swift attack spread like wildfire in some parts of Nhomlaau town, sowing seeds of uncertainty regarding the assailants' motives. Particularly, panic seized the marketplace while much of the city remained blissfully, yet terrifyingly, ignorant of the impending doom. Unlike others in town, Joseph Loi stood firm outside his home, his outward calm a stark contrast to the escalating internal dread that consumed him. Although he counted on the protection of powerful allies, their backing felt insufficient, a nagging worry in the recesses of his mind. He recognised the haphazard defences, leaving the bank and his family tragically exposed to a decisive assault by Duomduom's rash youth. A cloud of dread hung heavy in the air.

Unaware of the impending doom, the Nhomlaau people lived in serene tranquillity. Their idyllic existence, however, masked a terrifying vulnerability. The ravenous Duomduom youth, harbouring a malevolent intent to annihilate them, were poised to strike. This blissful unawareness rendered the Nhomlaau people utterly defenceless against the meticulously crafted assault. As they continued their daily tasks, oblivious to the gathering storm, a tangible tension, born of unseen menace, hung heavy in the air. The treacherous threat of the Duomduom's destructive ambition loomed, a hidden predator stalking its unsuspecting prey.

As news of the attack reached many parts of the town, Nhomlaau braced itself. The looming attack cast a chilling shadow over the town, its imminence a profound weight on every citizen. Only days remained before the anticipated onslaught, plunging the populace into a whirlpool of anxiety. Speculation ran rampant, a chaotic storm of rumours. Some whispered that the violence targeted solely the influential banker Mr. Joseph Loi. Others, however, found such a calamitous assault inexplicably vast, a monumental undertaking seemingly out of proportion to a single victim. With each sunrise, the growing terror solidified, leaving a chilling legacy of apprehension that poisoned every facet of Nhomlaau's existence.

As the tension and fear continued to escalate, the townspeople began to question the safety and the security measures in place. They first couldn't understand why the Duomduom inhabitants would want to attack their peaceful town. Some even started to doubt the rumours, wondering if it was all just a ploy to create chaos and fear. However, as the day of the attack drew closer, the fear and uncertainty only intensified, leaving the townspeople on edge and constantly looking over their shoulders.

Unbeknownst to them, their foe was not the sole danger they faced. Within their fortress, a reality of two realms was unfolding. One side was occupied by the wealthy and influential, basking in opulence and disregarding the plight of the common folk. On the other hand, a silent struggle for survival persisted as they battled against a world that seemed set against them. Despite the lavish surroundings, a sense of darkness lingered within the fortress walls, a constant reminder of the harsh realities faced by those on the other side. The stark contrast between the two worlds was a stark reminder of the divide that existed within their own home.

Suspicion hung heavy in the air, a chilling mist born of impending doom that poisoned neighbourly relations. The town's paralysed leadership finally jolted into action and scrambled to erect a desperate bulwark against the threat, but their efforts were obstructed by pervasive mistrust. A fragile yet tenacious spark of hope remained. A clandestine cell of defiant souls plotted rebellion, their bravery a defiant flame against the encroaching shadows, as they prepared themselves for the inevitable storm.

Panic continued to commandeer the Nhomlaau people. Their gazes often frantically scanned the overbearing confines, desperately seeking an escape, a single ray of salvation from their impending doom. The encroaching walls, a suffocating vice, offered no reprieve. Only their ragged gasps punctuated the agonising stillness, a silence heavy with dread. Existence itself seemed suspended, trapping them in a cage of stark, paralysing fear.

The growing fear later united the inhabitants of Nhomlaau town in a way that nothing else could. They were no longer divided by their differences but bound together by the shared experience of facing an uncertain fate. They had been living in two separate worlds, but the cloud of ignorance had been lifted, and now they were all in the same world, facing the same fate. At that moment, their individual stories merged into a tale of two worlds colliding.

As the people of Nhomlaau town awaited their impending doom together, regardless of their statuses, they couldn't help but reflect on the lives they had constructed, the loved ones they cherished, and the uncertain future that lay ahead. The storm was not only a physical force, but it also took a toll on their mental and emotional states. They were torn between hopelessness and resilience, unsure of how to confront the inevitable. Some came to terms with their destiny, while others were determined to battle until their final breath.

As fear would dictate, the people in Nhomlaau began to hear the imaginary sounds of fighting in the distance, breaking through the silence, jolting everyone out of their thoughts. The attack seemed to have begun. The storm had reached its peak, unleashing its fury upon the town. The roar of the wind and the crash of thunder echoed through the streets, drowning out any other sounds. It was a symphony of chaos, leaving the townspeople trembling in fear.

A murmur of apprehension rippled through Joseph's colleagues. Mr. Loi was called by his first name, Joseph, sometimes by his colleagues. Occasionally, they would call him by his last name,

Mr. Loi. They subtly warned of his opulent lifestyle as a banker, which marked him as a vulnerable target in Nhomlaau's precarious social landscape. Yet, he dismissed their anxieties with a wave of his hand, his faith in his rectitude unshakeable. Ignorantly clinging to this self-assuredness, Joseph disregarded the accumulating indications of danger. This firm conviction, however, bordered on reckless delusion. The warnings intensified, evolving into a chorus of urgent cautions, foreshadowing a gathering storm he was woefully unprepared to weather. His intransigence, ultimately, might prove catastrophic.

Joseph's steadfast resolve was a profound reflection of his integrity. Undeterred by potential repercussions, he remained unwavering in his convictions and self-belief. His solitary stand, a signal of fortitude and resilience, underscored the often-isolated nature of moral rectitude. The tangible intensity of his commitment to principle was almost physically felt, a potent force emanating from his unwavering spirit. This exceptional quality distinguished him, igniting in others a passionate desire to pursue their ethical imperatives.

The elders in Nhomlaau recognised the unshakeable nature of Mr. Loi's convictions. They often told those who did not know him very well that his beliefs were firmly entrenched in his very being. He remained impervious to external influence, resolutely clinging to his principles despite overwhelming pressure. This steadfastness frequently ignited intense conflicts with dissenters, resulting in bitter disputes and profound disagreements. Unyielding, he persevered despite condemnation and social isolation.

Despite being a gifted and ethical young man, Mr. Loi's conceit and inflexibility had always hindered him. The town elder, who had known him since childhood, had long harboured concerns that Mr. Loi's stubbornness would one day jeopardise the entire town. As the elders implored him to consider their perspectives, they couldn't help but feel disillusioned. They had always held out hope that he would evolve and become more receptive, but it appeared that his mindset was firmly entrenched.

Not just Nhomlaau shuddered under the weight of crippling fear; Duomduom's people were trapped in a living nightmare. Exhaustion gnawed at them, relentless vigilance their only defence against an uncompromising tide of dread. Each dawn brought a desperate scramble for existence, their lives a fragile dance on the precipice of annihilation. The omnipresent threat of Gutgook and his brutal henchmen cast a suffocating shadow of despair, crushing their hope. Their once-peaceful village now bubbled with suppressed rage and the ever-present threat of violence. Their taut nerves stretched to their absolute limit and threatened imminent collapse.

Gutgook's sudden absence cast a chilling despair over Duomduom, its once lively atmosphere replaced by a choking dread. The mystery surrounding his enigmatic undertaking fuelled a simmering apprehension, threatening to engulf the village's future in darkness. Deceptive tranquillity masked the villagers' overpowering anxieties. They harboured deep misgivings about the ramifications of Gutgook's reckless enterprise, particularly the unchecked power of his unruly followers. Doubt, a corrosive poison, eroded their serenity. A substantial unease, thick as the jungle mist, hung heavy in the air as they anxiously awaited his return, clinging to fragile hope while bracing for the inevitable storm. The jungle's stillness, pregnant with unspoken dread, amplified their fears more profoundly than any whispered rumour.

The once-proud and united villagers now lived in a state of constant trepidation. A profound dread permeated the village, chilling even the children's hesitant games. Their laughter, thin and brittle, was punctuated by watchful silences. Suspicion, a venomous cloud, stifled every interaction. Instead of joyous chatter, anxious murmurs slithered through the community, eroding the bonds of trust like relentless acid. The villagers huddled together, their desperate unity a flimsy embankment against an unseen enemy. Malicious gossip, spreading like a contagion, amplified their despair, severing their connection to any outside solace. Despair threatened to engulf them, yet a stubborn spark of defiance still glowed.

Meanwhile, Gutgook and his gang lived without any worries or concerns. They revelled in their authority and dominance over the villagers, seemingly deriving pleasure from their suffering. They were oblivious to the pain and torment they had inflicted, living in their isolated world of ignorance. The villagers were left to wait in uncertainty as Gutgook and his gang indulged in the liberties they had been cruelly denied.

Mr. Loi's greed had driven the youth of Duomduom's village under Gutgook's leadership to the brink of a cliff. His heartless exploitation ignited their suppressed rage, and they acutely felt the bite of Mr. Loi's oppressiveness. Their scheme, forged in underground meetings and shared resentments, solidified. Every attempt to postpone their action only hardened their determination. The imperturbable loveliness of Nhomlaau concealed a perilous undertow; an impending catastrophe threatened to obliterate its tranquil appearance.

Unlike the younger generation, the Duomduom village elders possessed a more nuanced perspective on the impact of Nhomlaau's entrepreneurs, viewing their activities with a less judgmental eye. While suspicions lingered—some businesspeople, like Mr. Loi, were suspected of surreptitiously pilfering milk from their herds in Duomduom village—the elders acknowledged the undeniable improvements his enterprise had brought. Mr. Loi's contributions included the provision of vital medical supplies, a philanthropic gesture that significantly enhanced the village clinic's capacity to combat malaria and deliver high-quality healthcare services. The doctor, empowered by this generous donation, was thus able to provide more effective preventative care and treatment.

Years of relentless affliction from the pervasive disease had ravaged the village, but a transformative shift arrived with readily available medicine and comprehensive preventative education. The previously overwhelmed physician, who had once battled insurmountable odds in delivering adequate care, was now empowered to serve the community. The agonising fear of losing loved ones to preventable illnesses finally subsided, replaced by a substantial sense of relief. This profound improvement bolstered the villagers' physical health and ignited a revitalised spirit, fostering a hopeful vision for the future.

Nevertheless, no persuasion from the village elders could sway the young people's scepticism. They methodically assessed the costs and benefits of Nhomlaau's business people's philanthropy, consistently finding themselves on the losing side of the equation.

Despite their tender years, these burgeoning adults displayed an astuteness far beyond their age. They acutely perceived the insidious exploitation inherent in Mr. Loi's enterprise, and their resolve extended beyond mere confrontation; they envisioned a fundamental, enduring shift in their village's fortunes. The youths understood the inherent unsustainability of Mr. Loi's charitable gestures, recognising them as a deceptive painkiller, camouflaging a future of deepening misery and subjugation.

The youth's defiance of Mr. Loi's corrupt regime was resolute, their unity a formidable force against his tyranny. This unwavering commitment ignited a flame of resistance within the community, inspiring widespread participation in the impending battle. Their boldness and solidarity served as an inspiration, illuminating the path to justice. Their resolute spirit, a compelling manifestation of hope, infused the town, galvanising others to join their cause. Their courageous stand against injustice became a powerful aroma of impending retribution, challenging the powerful and rallying the village youth to oppose Mr. Loi's despicable schemes.

Amidst a volatile blend of rage and nervousness, Gutgook keenly scrutinised the Duomduom youths' divergent reactions. Their conflicting responses posed a severe challenge to his authority. A faction of impetuous youths openly hatched schemes for immediate retribution, their whispers promising swift and brutal vengeance. In contrast, a more measured group advocated for prudence and calculated action. This internal discord threatened to shatter their fragile cohesion, yet Gutgook understood their combined might was paramount to confronting the looming danger. He required a decisive strategy and a unifying vision to galvanise them.

Driven by unwavering resolve, Gutgook's courageous spirit propelled him forward on his perilous journey. Ignoring the village elders' dire pronouncements, he stood firm in his intent to challenge Mr. Loi. The weight of his people's fate pressed heavily upon him as he departed, a crushing responsibility he bore with grim acceptance. He knew his actions risked catastrophic repercussions for the village, yet his duty as a leader compelled him to shield his community from oppression —a defiant stand against injustice. This bold decision fractured his bonds with the elders, who saw him as rash and foolhardy, and alienated friends who were apprehensive of the looming retribution. Yet, Gutgook's conviction remained unshaken; his course, though fraught with peril, was undeniably righteous.

Fuelled by simmering indignation, the youth rallied behind Gutgook, viewing him as a liberator from the elders' unwavering fealty to the tyrannical Mr. Loi. His audacious resistance sparked a conflagration of revolt. This overt defiance threatened the entrenched power structure, creating a volatile climate pregnant with the potential for societal fracturing. The elders' intransigence inadvertently bolstered Gutgook's influence, transforming him into a symbol of change. Gutgook's daring stratagem, though fraught with peril, presented a vision of a more just society, directly confronting the corruptible system and its acolytes. The escalating tension was unmistakable, a thunderstorm gathering on the horizon.

However, despite Gutgook's efforts, he could not shake off the tight grasp of anxiety. His conscience, weighed down by the consequences of his choices, was a constant companion that refused to let go. It was like a two-edged sword, relentlessly reminding him of the potential repercussions of his decisions. He was faced with two paths, each with its own set of consequences, and Gutgook knew that whichever one he chose, he would carry its weight for the rest of his existence. Every decision felt like a burden dragging him down, and he yearned for the freedom to act without the weight of morality.

Gutgook's conscience was not just a burden to bear. It was also a guiding light, reminding him of the delicate balance between right and wrong. As he struggled with the weight of his conscience, he knew that it would ultimately lead him to the path of righteousness, no matter how difficult it may be.

Paranoia choked the village, and its once-friendly atmosphere was replaced by venomous distrust. Accusations, like darts, were flung recklessly, igniting a raging inferno of dissension. Entrenched in their power, faction chiefs ruthlessly struggled for supremacy, as provisions that were previously abundant devolved into fiercely contested spoils, sparking bitter rivalry. The village teetered on the brink of collapse. Its destiny was shrouded in the ominous shadow of escalating strife. A path to reconciliation remained frustratingly obscure.

A chasm of incomprehension yawned between the generations. The formerly unified community fractured irrevocably and lay shattered. Leaders, intransigent in their respective belief systems, demonstrated a steady refusal to negotiate. Their perspectives, opposed, existed in isolated spheres, rendering them mutually invisible.

The consequences of the division among the factions of the Duomduom people were bound to be catastrophic. Some keen villagers, alongside those undergoing training in the jungle, lamented that their once tranquil and harmonious community was now plagued by strife and turmoil. Mutual trust among the villagers had dissipated, leaving a constant sense of tension and unease.

One night, the elders' aspirations for a harmonious settlement between Duomduom and Nhomlaau were crushed when they learned that Gutgook and his loyalists had departed from the jungle training centre and set off towards an undisclosed destination. With their palms sweating, they strained to find a solution. The weight of their responsibility burdened them, and their trembling hands reached out imaginatively to touch the delicate ties that bound the two worlds together. The elders could only hope to navigate through the chaos and restore the harmonious connection between Duomduom and Nhomlaau.

After some consideration, the elders informed the Executive Chief that the young people had departed from the training centre in the jungle for an unknown purpose. The news was first brought to them by a youth who had managed to escape and inform the village. The Executive Chief requested the youth's father to bring him before the chiefs in hopes of obtaining more details. However, by the time the boy's father tried to reach him, he had already returned to his original location.

Before the chiefs could act, news of the youths' departure from the jungle training centre quickly spread throughout the village like a raging inferno. After intense discussions, the chiefs determined that they must alert the residents of Nhomlaau to the potential threat posed by the youth of Duomduom. One of the chiefs was dispatched to Nhomlaau to notify the mayor of the impending danger.

Upon receiving the news, the mayor of Nhomlaau promptly took action, convening a meeting with his top administrators the following day. As a leader, the mayor prioritised the safety and well-being of his people above all else. At the meeting, the mayor and his team implemented various security measures to safeguard the community. One notable location under police surveillance was Mr. Loi's home.

The mayor's decision was met with a level of apprehension. Many in the town had lived in peace for so long that they had grown accustomed to its tranquillity, and because of this, news of an impending danger was not something they were prepared to face. Some began to question the validity of the mayor's claims, wondering if he was perhaps acting out of personal gain or ulterior motives. However, there were others in the Nhomlaau community who had long suspected that something was amiss. These individuals were relieved that the mayor had finally acknowledged the issue and hoped this would lead to a resolution. They were willing to trust in the mayor's judgment despite the doubts of others.

The surveillance of Mr. Loi's residence caused a deep divide within the town, leading to the formation of two distinct factions, each with its speculations and beliefs. Some alluded to Mr. Loi's substantial affluence and influence as the reason for his potential targeting by Duomduom youth. In contrast, others assumed his guilt based on his surveillance by the authorities. There were allegations of Mr. Loi's involvement in illicit activities, along with theories of him being a mere victim of circumstance. As debates raged on, a clear line was drawn between those who supported Mr. Loi and those who deemed him guilty.

As the day wore on, the discussions shifted towards the looming threat of an attack on the town. It became increasingly apparent that the young residents of Duomduom were making their way towards Nhomlaau town like a gathering storm. Their intended target remained shrouded in uncertainty, like a hidden dagger waiting to strike.

Chapter Six

The atmosphere in Nhomlaau was a dark cloud looming over the town, heavy with the weight of fear and dread. The town's citizens awaited the ruthless youths' arrival with bated breath, like prey anticipating the arrival of their predators. Tales of their brutal nature had spread like wildfire, filling the people with a sense of foreboding and dread. As the townspeople prepared for the Duomduom youths' arrival, it was as if they were preparing for a battle against a formidable foe, armed only with their wits and courage.

Even the typically fearless Nhomlaau police, their eyes displaying a flicker of apprehension, revealed a shared vulnerability. Their courage, usually a fortress, crumbled under the overbearing weight of despair. They were adrift, a vessel overwhelmed by a merciless tide of hopelessness, sinking beneath the crushing burden of their plight. A suffocating gloom, thick with the agony of their struggle, enveloped them entirely.

A gale, ferocious as a legion of demons, clawed at the town, its condescending fingers rattling windows and threatening to rip homes from their moorings. Denser than the thunderstorm, a substantial dread settled upon the terrified populace. Trapped within their dwellings, the townspeople trembled, their collective terror a tangible force amplifying the storm's savage power. Gaslight flickered, casting outrageous, elongated shadows that writhed and contorted in time with the wind's frenzied dance. The domineering darkness pulsed with a malevolent intelligence, its gaze unwavering, menacing. Beneath the storm's chaotic fury, an unspeakable evil stirred.

Nhomlaau's inhabitants faced the onslaught with vastly contrasting levels of protection. Some dwellings, with mud walls offering negligible resistance to gunfire, were cruelly exposed. Others, constructed of flimsy bamboo, presented equally fragile defences. In stark contrast, a fortunate few resided behind formidable concrete barriers, their properties ringed by fortified concrete fences further enhanced with razor wire and electrified strands—a bristling demonstration of privilege and security.

The town of Nhomlaau grimly represented societal inequality. Deep shadows of poverty enveloped the town, unambiguously juxtaposing opulent mansions against a sea of wretchedness. A privileged elite luxuriated in extravagant excess, their lives an outlandish misrepresentation of the relentless struggle endured by the vast majority. Dilapidated huts, clinging precariously to the edges of the town, housed the impoverished masses, forced into ceaseless toil serving their opulent masters.

Magnificent edifices, monuments to opulence and authority, provided no solace to the impoverished populace. A pervasive, thick and stifling dread choked the air. Meanwhile, the affluent remained serenely detached, their lives proceeding uninterrupted within fortified estates and behind impassable barriers. Their unsympathetic disregard strengthened the flames of rebellion. This chasm of inequality only heightened the tension preceding the inevitable conflict—a brutal struggle between the entitled and the desperate. The town's destiny teetered on the brink of catastrophe.

The people of Nhomlaau town were unprepared for what was coming. They knew whatever lay ahead would be difficult, but they were ready to face it together. Each challenge would test their strength, beliefs, and very existence. Yet, they stood firm, facing every new challenge with unwavering resolve.

A deafening silence engulfed the youths of Duomduom as they marched toward the town. The only sound that echoed through the air was the steady beat of their hearts as they summoned the fortitude to persevere. Their silence was broken only by the sound of their footsteps as they marched towards their targets. With each step, they grew stronger, their spirits lifted by the chorus of their unwavering determination. The struggle they faced would become their anthem, a reminder of their resilience and unbreakable bond.

As terror continued to grip the people of Nhomlaau and Duomduom, the youths of Duomduom moved stealthily through the jungle darkness, their senses sharp and vigilant. The air was thick with the scent of soil and vegetation, concealing their presence. Their unwavering determination to fight for their cause drove them forward despite the dangers. Under the cover of night, they inched closer to the banker's house, their murmured words barely audible. Shrouded in darkness, their identities remained a mystery.

The youths' collective yearning for the banker's mansion eclipsed all previous discord. With its grasping thorns and treacherous trails, the hostile thicket only served to temper their unwavering purpose. A deep interdependence blossomed amidst the hazardous expedition; each member's expertise was crucial to their collective safety. Tales of imminent peril sharpened their focus, intensifying their drive. The imposing banker's residence loomed before them, a siren's call promising unimaginable influence and devastating risk.

Overbearing humidity clung to the dense, bright green wall of the jungle, heightening the youths' apprehension. Every whisper of foliage, every brittle twig's fracture, galvanised the young adventurers, honing their senses to a razor's edge. Their clandestine objective ignited an unwavering resolve. A fleeting exchange of gazes sealed their commitment, a silent oath sworn amidst nature's untamed heart. The path forward remained mysterious, but their bravery blazed a defiant flame against the encroaching night. Despite the perilous terrain, their determination remained absolute.

Fuelled by their parents' agonising plight and the banker's heartless disregard, the Duomduom youth forged a daring plan. Their simmering anger, a crucible of injustice, hardened into resolute willpower. This unshakeable resolve propelled them toward exposing Mr. Loi's depravity despite the imminent risks. They acutely grasped the potential dangers. Time, a relentless adversary, sharpened their focus as they meticulously plotted their assault on the banker's opulent estate, driven by an enthusiastic desire to see him arrested and brought to justice. Their youthful rebellion ignited a spark of hope against the crushing weight of endemic corruption.

Stealthily, the Duomduom youths crawled towards the banker's house's back, each step measured, each posture controlled. A sparkle of movement—a silhouette hunched over a wavering lamplight, painstakingly tallying wads of banknotes—registered in one youth's sharp gaze. Their target was located. Days of gruelling discipline manifested in their flawlessly coordinated advance. This was their apex moment.

Unaware, the banker precisely tallied the banknotes, his methodical actions a jarring countermelody to the escalating terror surging outside. His concentration was unwavering, a stark juxtaposition to the burgeoning pandemonium. Perspiration glistened on the conspirators' foreheads. Their pulses pounded, a desperate demonstration accompanying their anxious vigil. Everything hinged on the element of surprise. The youths' cunning scheme, painstakingly devised, was about to face its ultimate trial.

The attacking youths were determined to get their hands on the banker and his money, as they had seen him counting his profits through the window. Their gaze was fixed on the banker's ill-gotten spoils, which resembled a predatory pack. The stench of his venality and inequity hung heavy in the air, igniting their fury. They convinced themselves they would not permit this sly financier to abscond with his corrupt earnings. Unwavering in their resolve to see him punished, the youth represented an unstoppable tide. Their intense, accusatory stares, sharp as shards of glass, penetrated the banker's carefully constructed façade of respectability, revealing the depravity beneath. His escape with his tainted wealth was simply unthinkable.

A patrolling pair of police officers, oblivious to the impending turmoil, stood near the banker's gate. A sharp-eyed assailant among the advancing youths sighted them. The news, relayed instantly to Gutgook, elicited a dismissive shrug. Weeks of painstaking preparation had strengthened these young rebels. This audacious manoeuvre was their calculated plan. Their hearts hammered a frantic rhythm as they cautiously approached their target, utterly unconcerned by the tranquil façade of the unsuspecting guardians. The impending clash between the two sides remained utterly imperceptible to the police officers, whose peaceful routine was on the verge of shattering into pandemonium.

Leading the group of young attackers was Gutgook, who wasted no time seizing a spear. Fully aware of the inferiority of their weapons against the officers' rifles, he charged towards one of them with a fierce determination. Gutgook's expertise with the spear was unmatched, and he knew he had to act quickly before the officer could fire. In a split second, he thrust his arm forward and unleashed the weapon, impaling the officer's chest as he collapsed to the ground, writhing in agony.

The second officer was like a swift hawk, ready to strike at the attackers, but they were like a well-oiled machine, trained and prepared for any sudden move. Their response to the officer's action was as precise as a clock, reflecting their military training. Like a symphony, they moved in perfect harmony, dropping to the ground as the bullets whizzed overhead. This was their routine in the jungle.

However, as one of the youths rose, the officer's bullets were like a relentless storm, mercilessly taking him down. He hit more youths who lay nearby. The situation was chaotic, with youth rolling to take cover behind anything they could see near them while the bullets from the officer dotted the ground almost everywhere.

Undeterred, Gutgook, the courageous champion, confronted the trigger-happy officer, a bulwark against the impending doom threatening his youth members. He'd already tasted victory, incapacitating one police officer. This only fuelled the surviving officer's fury. A torrential hail of gunfire rained down, a desperate bid to obliterate his adversary. Yet, Gutgook remained unyielding, an indomitable force against the ceaseless barrage. Each bullet swallowed by the earth represented a diminished danger to his people. His resolve, hardened by the conflict, grew as unwavering as an immutable peak defying a thunderstorm.

Gutgook's eyes scanned the chaotic battlefield, his vision clouded with gunpowder smoke. In the close distance, he could see the officer's figure, his uniform shining in the light. Gutgook's heart raced as he took in the devastation around him - the fallen colleagues, the splintered trees, the blood-stained ground. He knew he had to act fast.

The time was short. To survive and save his remaining colleagues from the angry police officer's bullets, Gutgook decided to take cover behind a tree. The tree's rough bark pressed against his back as he crouched behind it, trying to blend in with its trunk. He could feel the officer's presence growing closer and closer, his footsteps echoing in the silence. Gutgook's hands shook as he gripped his spear, ready to defend his friends. He knew the risks, but he couldn't just abandon them. He had to fight, no matter the cost.

In less than a minute after taking cover behind a tree, Gutgook's eyes locked onto the man in blue, his heart racing as the man drew closer. He could see the fear in his enemy's eyes, but he knew he couldn't back down now. The stakes were too high. As he sprinted towards the police officer, Gutgook's grip tightened on the spear, his knuckles turning wet with sweat that had never covered his whole body. He could feel the weight of the weapon, a familiar and reassuring presence in his hand. The wind whipped through his hair as he closed the distance between them, and he could hear the screams of his friends behind him.

As he neared the advancing police officer, Gutgook uttered a throaty cry and thrust his arm forward, releasing the spear with all his might. The weapon soared through the air, its sharp tip aimed directly at the chest of the officer. A scream of pain erupted from the man as the spear struck its mark, embedding itself deep into his flesh. Gutgook's heart leapt with a mixture of triumph and horror as he watched the officer fall to the ground. He turned to face the rest of the police, ready to fight until the very end.

Terror-stricken yet ignited by a surge of adrenaline, the Duomduom youth, momentarily paralysed by the hail of gunfire, erupted into action the instant they saw the second officer fall. A desperate resolve seized them; they surged towards the banker's heavily guarded mansion, their hands shaking with an unpredictable blend of fury and dread. Their advance was swift and merciless, fingers craving the icy grip of their weapons as they closed on their target. Each stride hammered home the moment's gravity; their pulses sore a frantic rhythm against their ribs. Fear, a tangible presence, only hardened their resolve to bring their nemesis to their knees.

As the young men approached the banker's house, they were met with a cacophony of gunfire echoing through the streets. The deafening sound filled their ears, causing them to instinctively cover their ears in an attempt to block it out. But it was the thick scent of gunpowder that truly assaulted their senses, making it hard to breathe. Gutgook, their leader, remained unfazed, his years of experience in battle showing in his every move. He calmly retrieved rifles from the deceased officers, not even flinching at the sight of their lifeless bodies. The sound of the guns may have been jarring, but to Gutgook, it was just another day on the battlefield.

An unstoppable tide of young ferocity crashed toward the banker's mansion. Their advance was a thunderstorm, brutal and unrelenting. Then, like bolts from the heavens, three additional law enforcement officers erupted onto the scene, their weapons spitting fire. The advancing youths scrambled for safety. But Gutgook, a veteran combatant, understood their predicament and ordered a counterattack. He found shelter behind a robust oak, his gaze steely. Trusting his survival to a single, desperate act, he placed a rifle into the trembling hands of his novice ally – their only hope against the relentless onslaught.

When Gutgook saw the fear in the youth's eyes, he realised he was the only one with any experience in handling firearms. He took cover behind a nearby tree and aimed his rifle. The sound of the gunshot echoed through the buildings, and he watched as one of the officers fell, his rifle slipping from his grasp. Gutgook knew that he had to keep firing.

Undeterred by the carnage, the surviving police officers toughened themselves. Their resolve hardened. They aimed to inflict brutal retribution upon the approaching mob. Gutgook, however, intended to eliminate the remaining law enforcement officers – a swift, decisive end. His second volley of shots, however, proved inaccurate. One officer, his instincts screaming, evaded the hail of bullets and took off toward the near darkness, his partner swiftly following.

Additional police officers surged onto the scene, their firepower intensifying the deafening barrage. A ferocious exchange of gunfire erupted, and a deadly ballet of light and shadow played out amidst the commotion. Projectiles ripped through the air, bouncing off the unforgiving stones and shattering window glass in a destructive upsurge. Terrorised civilians fled, desperately seeking sanctuary from the lethal storm of bullets. The pungent aroma of burnt propellant hung heavy in the air, starkly demonstrating the conflict's brutal escalation.

A hundred and twenty seconds passed. Then, the law enforcement officers vanished, melting into the inky blackness of the alley. Gutgook, lungs burning, pursued their fading forms, his heart a frantic hammer against his breastbone. The bitter sting of failure ignited a volcanic rage within him. He lunged forward, his hand closing on a brutal instrument, which he then pressed forcefully into his comrade's grasp.

Pressed for time, Gutgook commanded the young men to breach the banker's dwelling. A tangible sense of crisis hung heavy in the air as they confronted the bolted doors of the house, imposing obstacles seemingly challenging to their untrained hands. Undeterred, Gutgook spearheaded the attack. With a shattering crash, one of the windows of the banker's mansion yielded to their desperate force, adrenaline surging as they infiltrated the building in rapid succession. A triumphant thrill coursed through them; they had overcome the first hurdle, and their resolve hardened to fulfil their hazardous objective. Facing the uncertain terrors within, their courage and commitment shone incandescently bright.

After forcefully entering the banker's mansion, the youths sought the chamber where they'd witnessed his flamboyant display of riches. Nevertheless, a chilling emptiness greeted them. The room lay desolate, and their anticipated confrontation vanished. A bitter wave of frustration consumed them—their audacious plan thwarted, their moment irrevocably lost.

One of the youths, determined to salvage something from their failed attempt, got out through the broken window and looked up. He saw the banker's wife, a whirlwind of frantic activity, cramming precious possessions into a leather satchel. The scene was a representation of impending doom. Her desperate struggle mirrored the frantic efforts of a drowning sailor battling a tempestuous sea. Nonetheless, the sudden appearance of the youth acted as a stark illumination, instantly arresting her feverish actions. Terror, raw and unveiled, flooded her features, erupting in a shriek that pierced the night.

The youth was taken aback by the banker's wife's sudden reaction. He immediately rushed inside and informed his colleagues. They swiftly started making their way upstairs. The dark wooden stairs creaked under their weight. The youths' hearts raced as they approached the top, bracing themselves for what they might find. The musky scent of sweat and fear lingered in the air, causing their noses to crinkle in disgust.

Steel glinted menacingly, seizing the young men's attention. A threatening figure approached, his shadow a sinister, lengthening spectre. Fear constricted their throats. The firearm, cold and weighty in his grip, spoke volumes of practised lethality. His actions were precise, hostile, and horrifying. Hope for flight vanished. The youths ran back downstairs quickly. They tried to hide in the corner of the lobby.

Huddled together, the youths murmured frantic strategies, their gazes darting desperately toward the alley's inky maw. The atmosphere throbbed with dreadful suspense.

Amid the chaos, the youths couldn't help but feel a sense of regret and guilt. What had started as a harmless adventure to find and kill a wealthy unarmed banker had quickly turned into a dangerous and potentially deadly situation. They realised the harsh reality of the world they lived in. They were just pawns in a bigger game, disposable and insignificant.

While the terrified young men huddled, Gutgook remained in the initial chamber, painstakingly investigating the space beneath the bed for the financier. His preternatural cunning allowed him to anticipate consistently, and his pursuit was guided by the thunderous report of the firearm reverberating down the corridor.

Vigilant, Gutgook ascended the staircase, his gaze a hawk's, searching for threats. Reaching the landing, he saw the assailant, a figure of lethal intent, advancing on the gathering in the lounge. The rifle, menacingly levelled, spoke of cold calculation. The gunman moved with predatory grace, but Gutgook, a seasoned protector, was not surprised. In a flash of lethal precision, he neutralised the threat, his actions swift and decisive. A wave of collective gratitude washed over the group; their safety was inextricably linked to Gutgook, their unwavering guardian, who always anticipated danger and was ready to defend them.

The search continued as the youths' steps thundered through the vacant halls. Every room they entered was just as barren and lifeless, intensifying their sense of urgency. The once-grand mansion now lay empty, a mere shell filled with eerie silence.

Unfazed by the unsettling environment, the youths continued their investigation relentlessly. Every room in the mansion underwent rigorous scrutiny, each step feeling like a perilous manoeuvre through a labyrinthine structure. However, the revelation of a concealed passage ignited a spark of optimism amidst the mansion's shrouded mysteries. It served as a guiding light, drawing them inexorably toward their objective.

Suddenly, the sounds of footsteps marching from various directions towards the youth's location interrupted their planning. Terror, icy and acute, shattered their strained quiet. A surge of dread threatened to consume them. They frantically assessed the avenues of retreat.

Chapter Seven

A monument to avarice and ambition, the banker's mansion displayed an ostentatious opulence that inflamed the envy of his peers. Its lavish décor, a tapestry of extravagant details and luxurious comforts, was a deceptive suppression. Gleaming marble floors, mirroring the banker's immense fortune under the brilliance of cascading crystal chandeliers, masked a profound and gnawing disquiet. Concealed behind seemingly safe bookshelves, a labyrinthine network of secret passages descended into an underground escape route.

Driven by a fierce loyalty to his family, the banker painstakingly prepared for the impending crisis. He understood the gravity of the danger, the potential for catastrophic loss, and the absolute necessity of their survival. His comprehensive risk analysis left no possibility unexplored, and every contingency was thoroughly addressed. This unwavering dedication to his loved ones fuelled his relentless efforts, transforming his house into a fortress of protection against the encroaching threat. He was determined, at any cost, to ensure the family's safety.

The banker's careful precautions proved to be his family's deliverance. As his wife frantically gathered precious belongings, a glimpse of a menacing intruder through the window sent her sprinting to his side. "My love," she gasped, her voice trembling, "they've infiltrated the building! I saw a villainous assailant on the ground floor. We must escape immediately. Our lives are in imminent danger."

A chilling dread seized the children as their mother's normally soothing voice crackled with stark alarm. The menace was tangible, a suffocating presence in the strained quiet. Their expressions revealed a distressing picture of fright, bewilderment, and raw defencelessness. The crushing burden of imminent catastrophe pressed down on their tiny frames. A hushed supplication, a desperate invocation for safety against the unseen peril, trembled from the daughter's lips. The agonising suspense, thick and suffocating, paralysed them in fearful expectation. Terror gripped them all, a shared agony reflected in their troubled eyes.

The banker's pulse thundered, a frantic signal against the encroaching pandemonium. His spouse held their children close, their unspoken anguish a stark counterpoint to the rising dread. The escape route was uncertain. The banker couldn't fathom the peril lurking beyond the walled enclosure. He believed their relentless pursuers were almost upon them. He surveyed the clandestine passage, a desperate, high-stakes manoeuvre in their struggle for existence, its shadowy depths both menacing and alluring, offering a precarious ray of hope.

A cacophony of sporadic gunfire and frantic footfalls shattered the banker's composure, abruptly replaced by an unnerving silence. The crushing weight of the lone guard's valiant, yet ultimately unsuccessful, defence descended upon him. Paralysed, he stood, the grim reality searing itself into his consciousness: their solitary bulwark against the encroaching menace had fallen. The acrid tang of failure choked him.

With a sense of urgency, the banker swiftly guided his family through a hidden passageway and down a concealed elevator. The escape route was a covert exit in the perimeter wall, serving as their gateway to safety. He remained watchful, determined to protect his loved ones until the danger posed by the attacking youths was eliminated. He led them to the police headquarters in the heart of Nhomlaau town, ensuring their well-being.

"Sir," the banker gasped. Terror seized him; his voice was a barely controlled tremor beneath a calm façade. "The anticipated assault from the youth of Duomduom village is underway now, besieging my residence. My security guards have been annihilated. The enemy has breached the defences. My family and I, by a hair's breadth, fled through a concealed passage. Immediate, overwhelming support is paramount. This is a dire emergency. The aggressors are ruthlessly efficient and formidably equipped."

The banker's imperturbable pomposity crumbled; his customary composure had become a forgotten relic. His immaculate attire, now disarrayed, reflected the tempest raging within. His fingers, shaking violently, frantically sketched a crude plan, the charcoal smudged by his intense anxiety.

The police chief's soothing words were lost in the banker's terror. His ragged breathing, a thunderous percussion, dominated the room, silencing all else. The prior calmness had vanished, supplanted by a suffocating atmosphere of pandemonium and desperate haste.

Even though overwhelmed by stark terror, the banker was still brave enough to volunteer to guide the reinforcements. His offer was a desperate plea. His voice, a shaky whisper, and his hands convulsed with agitation betrayed his profound anxiety.

After some minutes of desperate pleas for help and the police chief's acceptance at the police headquarters to send the necessary police force, the banker frantically detailed a clandestine approach for the reinforcements, a plan born of sheer desperation to avert catastrophe. The air crackled with the substantial tension of his fear; the scent of sweat and dread hung heavy in the air. He understood the catastrophic repercussions of failure, yet his resolve to guide the police burned bright, starkly contrasting his visible fright.

The banker's suggestions galvanised the courageous police chief into immediate action. Terse orders, weighty with unspoken implications, radiated outward from the police chief to the unit commanders. The gravity of the situation—a brazen, violent assault perpetrated by the Duomduom youths, a fearless, well-armed, with rudimentary weapons gang—was substantial. The police chief's intolerance for such lawlessness left no room for equivocation. Acutely aware of this, the commanders swiftly implemented the chief's directives.

After consideration, a platoon was handpicked to launch an offensive against the armed youths who had seized control of the banker's property. Their efficiency was evident in their methodical armament checks and precise movements. With time ticking against them, they were determined to take action before it was too late. The platoon chosen for this mission comprised the most elite officers in the force, all of whom were eager to prove themselves in the face of this crisis.

The police chief's intense stare, a laser beam of scrutiny, locked onto the platoon. For minutes, his unwavering gaze demanded absolute obedience. Then, he planted himself before them, an embodiment of silent power that stilled their movements entirely. Though their postures were rigid, revealing nothing outwardly, a barely perceptible shudder exposed the tautness within. Their weapons, held at a hair's breadth from their braced legs, reflected a controlled fury. The guns, though seemingly relaxed, spoke volumes – poised, ready to spring into action. A tangible sense of suppressed energy charged the air, a volatile calm hanging heavy in the air. The platoon, a potent instrument of order, projected an excellent blend of strength and discipline, a predator poised for the kill.

"Attention!" The police chief's sharp command cut through the air. A synchronised, earth-shaking thud resonated as the platoon lifted and brought their left boots down hard, a display of immediate, unwavering obedience. Weapons were instantly secured – the barrels nestled in their right hands, left hands hanging limp, a stark picture of controlled readiness. "Your objective," he declared, his voice grim, "is the immediate eviction of the Duomduom gang from our banker's residence. Their unlawful occupation ends now. You will act swiftly and decisively. I expect a confirmation of mission success before you return here."

A substantial tension, woven from anxiety and steely determination, hung in the air as the commanding officer's scrutiny swept over the assembled group. The gravity of their impending mission pressed down, a suffocating weight on every shoulder. He emphasised the critical need for measured and deliberate responses, cautioning against impulsive acts that could ignite unforeseen chaos. Their purpose was unambiguous, yet flawless execution was vital. He invoked their sacred vow, their solemn duty to serve justice, even as they navigated the treacherous path of potential bloodshed. With his unwavering gaze upon them, the operation commenced, a slow, deliberate dance of precision.

"Move now and do your job as quickly as possible," a stark order from the police chief, short and decisive, shattered the strained quiet. Every officer in the platoon understood the perilous moment; grim resolve hardened their features, mirroring the chief's grave anxiety. A heavy expectancy settled over them as the units positioned, their movements honed to lethal precision, the product of relentless discipline. The operation loomed, a gathering storm.

While the catastrophe intensified, pockets of the city lay calm. A profound stillness, punctuated only by the whispered secrets of the wind through the foliage, stood in stark opposition to the pandemonium and devastation raging elsewhere. The city's naivete was substantial in its obliviousness to the unfolding tragedy. Unsuspecting of the malevolence hidden in the shadows, it revelled under the serene gaze of a celestial canopy.

A crushing burden of accountability weighed heavily on the officers tasked with leading the reinforcement platoon. Each element of their intricate design was paramount. They dissected the information provided by the banker with painstaking precision, anticipating every conceivable impediment. Driven by an unshakeable resolve, their concentration was absolute, a tacit pact binding them. Their audacious task weighed heavily, each manoeuvre fraught with consequence. Unwavering in their commitment, they were engrossed, bound by a silent communion. Tactile sensitivity became their compass, directing their every action.

Equipped with all available assets, the police embarked on their mission. The gang had barricaded themselves inside for about an hour and were not going to surrender easily. However, the determined police force had a powerful ally in their arsenal - the element of surprise. With the banker, a knowledgeable insider, leading the way, the police were confident.

The rhythmic thumping of the advancing police force's heavy boots reverberated through the deserted streets of Nhomlaau city, each impact a forceful declaration of authority. Their radio chatter, a static-laced torrent, underscored their unwavering vigilance. The metallic resonance of their badges, a constant, insistent chime, amplified their steadfast presence. Commands, crisp and unwavering, sliced through the night, their voices imbued with the weight of their sworn duty. Their unified power, a demonstrable wave of protection, was a stark reminder: they were the guardians of the city and its people.

As the police reinforcements advanced towards the banker's residence, the resounding clamour of metal grew louder. Despite the adrenaline coursing through their veins, they remained composed and level-headed, demonstrating the rigorous training they had received in handling such critical situations. The authoritative voices of their superiors reverberated in their minds, bolstering their bravery as they forged ahead.

With laser-like concentration, the officers advanced on the banker's sprawling property. The operation's outcome held the banker's family's future and their department's credibility in the balance. Their resolute commitment to upholding the law underscored their unwavering dedication to safeguarding their community.

As the police reinforcements approached the Duomduom youths who occupied the banker's mansion, many things ran through their minds. Their advance was a thunderous symphony of steel. At this point, the mansion occupants heard the oncoming sounds and were afraid inside the building. They were busy thinking about how to escape.

When the marching towards the occupied mansion gathered a swift pace, the platoon commander, a seasoned police officer, was profoundly struck by the banker's audacious spirit and sharp intellect. Usually unflappable, the banker's demeanour now radiated steely resolve. His mind was a whirlwind of tactical manoeuvres and contingency strategies. Each stride forward demonstrated his unwavering determination, a profound upsurge of defiance against the encroaching threat. He appeared convinced he would not surrender his ancestral home to the occupiers. The chance to reclaim it fuelled his every action.

The splintered glass, a stark demonstration of violent intrusion, pierced the banker's awareness. His pulse, a frantic drumbeat, reverberated through his chest. Only he perceived the platoon commander's cautious signal, a desperate appeal for decisive action. A frightening wave of apprehension washed over him. The increasing brightness from the mansion's security lights now hinted at a threat far surpassing their initial calculations. The broken window through which the attackers entered the mansion became clear, sending nerve-wracking effects down the marrow of the reinforced police officers. Swift, resourceful adaptation was paramount. Their meticulously crafted plan proved hopelessly insufficient.

A chill, usually inhabiting the banker's composed exterior, gave way to a jolt of pure adrenaline. He discreetly alerted the platoon commander; their unspoken exchange, born from decades of partnership, spoke volumes. Their combined expertise formed an imposing bulwark against the impending danger, a precisely orchestrated strategy to preserve order.

The police officers were already establishing a secure zone. The mansion loomed as a sinister silhouette against the night, a stage set for the impending showdown. Yet, even facing this formidable challenge, a flicker of optimism ignited within the banker. Their strategy, however, remained precarious, teetering on the edge of uncertainty, hostage to unforeseen circumstances.

The banker paused in one place. His eyes scanned the wall, aided by the dim streetlight near the mansion. He moved again. As they approached the attackers, his strategic mind was already at work, collaborating with the platoon commander to devise a plan of action. Together, they presented a formidable front, poised to overcome any obstacle in their path.

A relentless rhythm pounded—the platoon commander's boots kept landing on the stones and making screeching sounds, and he appeared not bothered, a counterpoint to the frantic drumming in his chest. Perspiration glistened on his forehead, starkly reflecting the men's collective dread. His eyes, sharp and vigilant, sliced through the murky recesses of the alleyways, hunting for even the slightest indication of the fugitive.

A substantial dread, dense as a shroud, enveloped the officers, a silent confrontation with an unseen enemy. Perspiration glistened on their foreheads, reflecting the moisture clinging to the muzzles of their firearms. The atmosphere throbbed with barely contained energy; each inhalation was a risky revelation. The elusive Duomduom youths, experts in camouflage and subterfuge, remained invisibly entrenched within the structure. The crushing burden of duty bore down on the advancing police reinforcements. The fate of countless civilians teetered precariously as they advanced into the brightening interior of the sprawling mansion.

As the banker and the police approached the mansion, the smell of freshly cut grass filled the air. Beneath the pleasant scent was a hint of something else—the sharp, metallic tang of fear. The banker's focus was solely on liberating his house from unjustified occupation, and the faint smell of danger that lingered in the air only fuelled his determination to free his mansion from the youth he accused of targeting him for no reason.

With masterful precision, the commanding officer marshalled his units into a perfectly horizontal line, each element precisely positioned according to its designated function. He politely directed the banker to withdraw, relinquishing control to the law enforcement officers. The banker, having already meticulously indicated the access points – the imposing gates and the imposing façade of the grand manor – had fulfilled his duty. The commanding officer, a strategic genius, organised the scene with unwavering authority.

The police platoon commander repeatedly emphasised that the assault on the banker's palatial residence demanded specialised skills. For this reason, he urged the banker's immediate evacuation, allowing the specialised police officers unfettered access to resolve the crisis. But the banker, deaf to the commander's impassioned entreaties, exhibited a stubbornness bordering on defiance. His firm resolve was a stark, defiant challenge to the commander's escalating anxieties, demonstrating his inflexible will.

The commander's fury boiled at the banker's intransigence. However, the immediacy of the perilous situation paralysed him. He could not attack the enemy and deal with the stubborn banker at the same time. At that moment of uncertain decision, a sudden, sharp insight pierced the murkiness of the platoon commander's frustration. He decided the banker's recalcitrance might prove a fortuitous element within their precarious operation. He chose, therefore, to let the banker remain unobstructed.

The platoon commander was right in his decision. The banker's deserved renown for shrewdness and ingenuity was undeniable. His painstaking foresight in anticipating threats had not escaped the commander's keen observation. Indeed, this meticulous nature had drawn the commander's sharp focus. A powerful alliance blossomed between them, forged on his understanding of the banker's critical role in safeguarding his family's well-being.

With officers deployed tactically around the structure, the platoon commander anticipated the perpetrator's every manoeuvre. His strategy seemed flawless, a testament to years of honed expertise. Still, a persistent unease gnawed at him; could he truly account for every contingency? The atmosphere crackled with anticipation; even the most insignificant unforeseen circumstance risked shattering the commander's painstaking preparations. He remained vigilant, his eyes locked on the building's inky apertures.

Facing an imminent threat, Gutgook's resourceful youth transformed their haven into a frantic stronghold. They improvised barricades from scavenged debris, a defiant demonstration of their unwavering resolve. Armed with meagre weapons and an abundance of determination, they occupied their positions, grim-faced and unyielding. Their temporary fortifications, woefully inadequate, were bolstered only by absolute, defiant courage. Yet, they stood firm, prepared to make their last stand, their sanctuary a final, bloody bastion.

The police units continued to march slowly forward, their presence looming over the area. Their stern faces and rigid movements signalled the severity of the situation. The young defenders stood their ground, their eyes wide with fear as they waited for the impending clash. The only sound was their panicked breaths, their trembling bodies a stark contrast to the stoic police units. It was a battle of wills, both sides bracing for the inevitable, brutal confrontation that was about to unfold. The world seemed to hold its breath, anticipating the clash between the two forces.

Inside the banker's compound, the youth positioned themselves at the entrances, their weapons ready. They knew that their enemy was near, and adrenaline was coursing through their veins. The sounds of spears and swords rubbing against one another echoed through the air, intensifying the tension. Gutgook's heavy footsteps matched the pounding of his heart as he took his place at the main gate of the banker's wall, his grip on his spear and gun tightening.

The discordant blend of noises formed a harmonious tune of preparedness, saturating the atmosphere with a sense of enthusiasm.

Amidst the disharmony, Gutgook's authoritative voice emerged, overpowering all other sounds with unwavering commands. The looming battle appeared substantial, its thunderous clamour consuming the senses.

Within two minutes of Gutgook and his followers taking their positions, the police surrounded the perimeter, hoping to enter through hidden gates that the banker had disclosed. However, the youths, who had already occupied the premises, had discovered and stationed themselves at all secret entrances long before the police could reach them.

Inside the compound, the shooting commenced. The police officers immediately dropped to the ground, then rose and charged towards the wall from various angles. The odour of fear mixed with the metallic scent of blood as they advanced towards the gate. The night sky was saturated with the fragrance of desperation as the intense clash between law enforcement and the Duomduom youth intensified.

At the secret gate on the left side of the building, the smell of gunpowder hung in the air. Fokosorot Two, positioned there, proved himself to be a fearless marksman, dispatching four law enforcement officers in two minutes. The remaining youths eagerly awaited their chance to strike, armed with spears and swords.

The police platoon commander's heart raced like a bullet as he surveyed the scene unfolding before him. His voice pierced through the deafening chaos, giving clear and concise orders to his officers. He stood as a beacon of guidance, urging his platoon to evacuate the area and safeguard as many lives as possible. The acrid stench of smoke only fuelled his urgency, compelling him to make decisions.

"Retreat from the barricade!" The platoon commander's thunderous bellow instantly filled the city streets and the mansion's walls, a stark order slicing through the clamour. His voice, fraught with desperate urgency, galvanised fear in every heart. The police obeyed the orders and withdrew from the banker's mansion. A wave of fear washed over them in distress. The command had resonated with them like a death knell, a foreshadowing of imminent peril.

The initial responders were the police officers stationed near the platoon commander. They had already been horrified as they watched Fokosorot Two take down their colleagues on the left side of the wall fence. As they fled from the scene, other units quickly dispersed in a frenzy. A sense of terror and chaos consumed them as they tried to escape.

Gutgook heard the call and commanded his men to charge out of the fence and attack the retreating police. The air was filled with the deafening sound of gunfire and shouts as Gutgook's men charged forward.

The police were taken aback and found themselves in a difficult situation. They had to think on their feet and quickly shift into defensive positions. They were vulnerable, like prey in the open.

Amidst the pandemonium, it felt like the air was charged with an electrifying energy. The scene resembled a bustling beehive, with everyone buzzing about in a chaotic frenzy, unsure of their next move. The sound of gunfire reverberated like a symphony; each shot was a distinct note in an unsettling melody. The sight of the fleeing police officers from afar was awe-inspiring as they scurried like ants in every direction, desperately trying to restore order amidst the turmoil.

Despite the platoon commander's thunderous voice echoing through the chaos, commanding the officers to halt their retreat and engage the rampaging youths in the open, the fleeing officers disregarded his orders. The youths had transformed into a frenzied horde, consumed by a thirst for retribution that clouded their judgment. Their battle cries grew louder, and their fury intensified.

The Duomduom youths, a raging torrent of ferocity under Gutgook's command, shattered the commander's defences. His fearless resistance, a solitary beacon against the onslaught, was ultimately futile. The police officers could not help their leader. Seeing his desperate struggle ignited panic among them. Their ranks fractured, their discipline dissolving into chaotic flight. The remaining police, hearts seized by terror, fought only for their survival. A gruesome aftermath marked their retreat: a landscape of slaughter punctuated by the commander's horrific, isolated end. After a harrowing struggle, the relentless barrage of Gutgook's merciless assault finally extinguished the platoon commander's life.

Gutgook's victory against the police reinforcements was instantaneous and pitiless. The banker's neighbours, now vulnerable and subjugated, cowered under the dreadful weight of his imminent savagery. Terror seized them as Gutgook's ferocious young warriors spread and commenced their methodical hunt, their menacing expressions foretelling severe punishment. Rumours of torment and demolition rippled through the banker's hiding neighbours, spreading like a contagion in the shadowed recesses of their homes, where they took cover.

The streets were filled with chaos and destruction as the angry mob chased their enemies into the dark of the night. During this madness, the banker stood his ground, fighting for his survival against all odds. He then winced as a scorching pain shot through his leg, the impact of the bullet sending him to the ground. Armed with a rifle provided by the authorities, he wielded it skilfully in defence. He could feel the weight of the weapon in his hands, his fingers gripping the cool metal tightly. Each movement was calculated as he fended off his assailants, determined to protect himself and his property.

As the night wore on, the situation grew more dire. The youths were everywhere, their numbers multiplying with each passing moment. The banker, already injured from the skirmish, was like a ship tossed around in a tempestuous sea. Despite his best efforts, he was unable to fend off the relentless attacks, and it was only through sheer luck that he was dragged to safety by a police officer who took him to a nearby unfinished wall fence.

The reek of incinerated rubble was a poignant reminder of the savagery that transpired. An overpowering, choking haze lingered, a caustic veil obscuring vision and rasping in lungs. The stillness, punctuated only by the sporadic hiss of dying flames, was more oppressive than the smoke itself, a suffocating blanket woven from devastation and untold agony. Amidst the wreckage, fragile remnants of lives – a child's discarded toy, a charred memento – lay scattered, poignant demonstrations of the brutal violence. The city braced for a desolate sunrise.

As the first light pierced the darkness, the raiding Duomduom youths had wholly disappeared, absorbed by the unforgiving expanse of the countryside. Nhomlaau, once vibrant with its boisterous energy, was now a ghost town, its streets eerily deserted. The town's usual bustling activity had been extinguished, leaving behind a chilling stillness. A substantial sense of emptiness hung heavy in the air, a suffocating silence that blanketed the forsaken settlement as if life had been brutally excised.

Despair choked the survivors of Nhomlaau as they witnessed the aftermath of the brutal assault by the youths of Duomduom village. Their simple, thatched homes were consumed by the relentless crossfire, leaving behind only charred remnants and crushed debris. The attack, a calculated act of viciousness, struck at the heart of their peaceful town. The residents, already vulnerable, felt the full weight of the Duomduom youths' merciless efficiency. Their flawless raid shattered Nhomlaau's defences with terrifying speed, leaving only hopelessness and shattered aspirations in its wake. The cold precision of the attack was profoundly unsettling.

Fuelled by righteous fury, the citizens of Nhomlaau scoured the ruins for the wounded, grim resolve hardening their features. The city's shared agony propelled a desperate, collective response. Amidst the pandemonium, a fragile spark of hope ignited as medics ministered to the casualties, their expert touch bringing a measure of comfort. Yet, dwindling resources intensified the pressure, underscoring the precariousness of their situation. Concurrently, the relentless pursuit of the perpetrators unfolded, a grim counterpoint to the city's frantic struggle for revival. Their implacable demand for retribution would not be easily satisfied.

Shared sustenance provided meagre solace amidst the catastrophic wreckage. A fragile glimmer of optimism ignited as community members of Nhomlaau town aided one another. Though bearing the wounds of trauma, the children discovered tranquillity in the innocent act of drawing their reimagined city, their art a vibrant expression of a hopeful tomorrow.

Chapter Eight

From the charred wreckage, smoke still snaked upwards, a stark symbol of the brutal conflict between police and the rampaging Duomduom youth. Terror clung to the townspeople, their hushed whispers recounting the night's horrors. Then, the jarring rumble of military vehicles shattered the silence. Soldiers' faces, imprinted with grim resolve, poured from the trucks into the devastated town square. Though offering a precarious promise of peace, their arrival couldn't erase the lingering despair. The unpleasant odour of destruction and fear permeated the air, suffocating the once-vibrant Nhomlaau. Overwhelmed by the chaos, the local government, desperate for order, had called in the army.

A tranquillity fell over the town as the soldiers established their defensive cordon. Sunlight glinted menacingly off their weaponry, projecting a worrying melancholy over the terrified populace. However, barely perceptible, a fragile spark of hope flickered within the citizens' fearful gazes. A profound duality gripped them: trepidation warred with a desperate yearning for deliverance. The soldiers' presence, while offering a splinter of cautious optimism, couldn't quite eclipse the pervasive dread that clung to their hearts like a shroud. Now a crucible of conflicting emotions, the town awaited its fate with a mixture of resignation and frantic hope.

Meanwhile, the dense, dark jungle shielded the fleeing youths, their intimate familiarity with the treacherous landscape providing a critical edge. Nevertheless, the stern military commander, his countenance grim, steadied his troops for the arduous chase. Their objective was the apprehension of the Duomduom youths—a daunting mission fraught with the challenges of unforgiving terrain and the rebels' ingenious tactics. The relentless pursuit commenced, the destiny of these defiant young souls hanging precariously in the balance.

The commander and his company marched into the jungle, their boots crunching on the undergrowth. Sweat dripped down their faces as they scanned the surroundings, on high alert for any signs of danger. The jungle was alive with the sounds of chirping birds and buzzing insects, but the commander's mind was focused. He squinted his eyes, trying to see through the thick foliage. The vibrant green leaves and twisted vines created a maze of shadows, making it difficult for the commander to spot any potential threats. He could feel the weight of duty on his shoulders, knowing that the lives of his men depended on his keen senses. Every step was calculated, every movement deliberate as they moved deeper into the unknown terrain.

"You who are on that flank," the commander's voice echoed in the ears of each soldier. The urgency of his words sent a chill down their spines. "Move as quickly as you can while taking precautions."

"Aye, aye, sir," the soldiers responded almost in unison. They were no longer ordinary men and women; they had been trained to endure any obstacle, fight, and survive.

As they moved deeper into the jungle, the commander's eyes darted from one tree to another, searching for any signs of movement. The green canopy above cast dappled shadows on the ground, making it difficult to spot any hidden enemies. The dense vegetation seemed to swallow them up, and the commander couldn't shake off the feeling of being watched, but he steeled his nerves, determined to carry out his duty and bring peace back to the town.

After a fruitless search for the attackers, the commander summoned platoon leaders from various flanks to hold a strategic session. As they assembled around him, the commander's eyes scanned the anxious faces, each man waiting breathlessly for orders. His gaze settled on Lieutenant Robinson, the leader of the second platoon, barely out of the officers' cadet corps. The Major cleared his throat with a gentle rasp.

"Lieutenant Robinson, do you know what we should do now that the assailants are nowhere to be seen?" the commander asked.

The young Lieutenant straightened his back, determination shining in his eyes. "Yes, sir. I suggest we split our forces into two groups, one to continue searching for the attackers and the other to go back to town to fortify the defences around key installations."

The Commander turned to Lieutenant Jerome of the first platoon and asked, "What do you think we should do now that the attackers are nowhere to be seen?"

The other lieutenants turned their attention towards Jerome, curious to hear his thoughts. He was a seasoned officer who had conducted many operations before. Jerome took a moment to collect his thoughts before responding to the commander's question. He knew that the enemy was still out there, and they needed a plan to flush them out.

"We should follow them into Duomduom village," responded

Lieutenant Jerome of the first platoon. "These attackers are youths from that village."

The other leaders nodded in agreement. A unanimous murmur of assent rippled through the assembled leadership. They agreed that the assailants had retreated to Duomduom. Pursuing them to their home, a decisive engagement within the village itself, represented the most effective—and reasonable—path to retribution.

"I am told that the Duomduom people have accused the townspeople of milking their cattle in the bush," said Lieutenant Joseph of the third platoon. "I cannot suspect any other person apart from the youth of Duomduom village for this reason."

The commander nodded approvingly and turned to the others. "We'll do as Lieutenant Jerome suggested. If they have all gone there, we must act quickly and follow the assailants into the village. You go back to your platoons and let us track the footprints of these attackers so we can catch up with them as quickly as possible." They vanished towards their platoons.

The commander, observing his officers' hasty return to their units, understood the precarious destiny of Nhomlaau town hung in the balance. His burden was to forge the soldiers' path to triumph. Moments later, with the meticulous control of an expert, he ordered the forces to move toward Duomduom village, intent on conducting a symphony of victory. He served as their unwavering protector, a bulwark against the encroaching storm threatening the town and its inhabitants. His guidance illuminated the company's way, an inspiration cutting through the chaos, ensuring their safe arrival at their target. A seasoned navigator charting a perilous course, the company commander believed he would lead the soldiers to ultimate victory.

The platoons began to move into their respective positions. The commander also became busy. He resumed the search for the assailants. He was a busy man, leading his troops through unforgiving terrain, resolute in his quest to find the culprits and bring them to justice. His heart raced as he contemplated the potential consequences if they failed to locate the attackers. With his bodyguards by his side, the commander pushed onward. His mind fixated on finding and halting the perpetrators before they could return and cause more damage to the town of Nhomlaau and its inhabitants.

Fear, a chilling shroud, enveloped the Duomduom raiders as they retreated from Nhomlaau. Their earlier bravado had evaporated, leaving behind a terrified band, hunted like deer by the approaching army. The echoes of their reckless assault on Nhomlaau still clawed at their minds, every rustle of leaves, every sigh of the wind, a fresh stab of panic. A desperate scramble replaced the once-proud stride, their arrogance replaced by a primal need to escape. A gathering gloom on the horizon – the ominous shadow of impending capture – ignited a fresh surge of terror. Their flight became a frantic, breathless race against what they rightly believed could be the approaching soldiers, their hearts pounding a frenetic rhythm of dread.

Hot on the heels of the Duomduom youths, the relentless soldiers pressed their pursuit. The troops' inexorable advance culminated at the village's perimeter as the young insurgents scrambled for sanctuary within Gutgook's stronghold, parched and desperate. A stampede of terrified villagers violently ended their brief reprieve, their faces etched with primal fear. The army's brutal invasion sundered the hamlet's tranquillity, transforming the peaceful settlement into a commotion of chaos as they ruthlessly hunted their quarry.

The ominous thud of military boots reverberated through the village square, a dreadful rhythm accompanying the soldiers' advance. Terror gripped the populace, its chilly fingers tightening on the hearts of both the aged and the innocent. A substantial atmosphere of dread hung heavy, and the villagers' whispers of impending brutality were a frightening premonition. Uncertain doom descended, casting a cloud over the land. Their flight was a frantic, desperate, chaotic scramble for survival as the shadow of the encroaching army blotted out hope, leaving only an agonising, uncertain future.

"What have you seen?" asked Fokosorot One.

"I witnessed the armed forces pursuing individuals to the right of us," replied a young person who had ventured into the pond to gather additional water for the group.

"Come quickly," barked Gutgook. "Let us not waste time. What do we do? Do we run away like the people running there, or should we fight these intruders?"

After a heated debate, the young people decided to face the oncoming army and defend their village. Gutgook devised a plan of attack. He ordered Fokosorot One to take the right flank and Fokosorot Two to take the left. Gutgook himself stood in the centre, taking the lead like a noble lion defending his territory.

Together, they were a tempest of blades and rage, a force to be reckoned with. With Gutgook's battle cry as their guiding force, the youth charged forward, a fierce and calculated assault against their enemies. Like a storm, they thought they were unstoppable. Their swords and shields were their weapons, with some of the few rifles that they captured from the police officers they killed during the attack on Nhomlaau. Yet, their determination was their best ally.

Paralysed by astonishment, the invading army watched, incredulous, as the fearless Duomduom youths advanced towards their position. Perspiration beaded on the soldiers' brows. The firm resolve blazing in the young combatants' eyes struck them with chilling force. With each stride of the approaching youths, the invaders' uncertainty deepened, a tangible weight in the air. Never before had they confronted such an indomitable spirit. The sun glinted off the youths' weapons, amplifying their valiant courage. Overwhelmed by the sheer audacity of these young warriors, the invaders recoiled, momentarily bereft of their composure.

The rigid formations of the invading army changed, dissolving into agile, independent fighting groups of platoons and squads. With decisive speed, each platoon established a dominant attacking perimeter. This dynamic tactical shift was crucial to neutralise the unpredictable danger presented by these unexpectedly youthful and ferocious attackers.

The two sides drew closer to each other. As they met, the air was thick with the sound of clashing weapons and the battle cry of the warriors. Gutgook stood in the centre, his eyes scanning the battlefield for any sign of weakness in the enemy's ranks. With his strategic forces split, he had set the stage for an epic clash between the two sides.

The young warriors kept charging forward, their adrenaline pumping and their hearts full of bravery. They were fighting for their village, families, and way of life. As they fought, their movements were fluid and coordinated. With every strike of their weapons, they defended their home and their people, willing to give their lives for the cause.

Outmatched and outgunned, the villagers' insignificant defences crumbled before the military's overwhelming might. Their bravery, though fierce, proved to be a tragically inadequate shield against the storm of superior weaponry and tactical expertise. Captured at great peril in Nhomlaau during the night attack, ten rifles for the youth of Duomduom proved a pathetically insufficient bulwark against the relentless assault against them.

The coordinated military advance swiftly crushed the vigorous resistance from the youth. As the brutal conflict unfolded, the villagers' tenacious spirit, though unwavering, succumbed to the grim reality of their impending defeat. Their future was cast into the bleak shadow of inevitable subjugation.

The past's lofty ambitions and virtuous goals were extinguished, supplanted by a brutal, visceral need for mere existence. Idealistic visions and noble pursuits, once their guiding stars, now flickered faintly in the recesses of memory, eclipsed by the harsh, unforgiving reality of a society ravaged by conflict and despair. Their courageous struggles proved futile against the relentless tide of destiny. Still, they persisted, clinging stubbornly to life amid unbeatable odds.

The military's overwhelming force obliterated the village's youthful resistance in a savage, five-minute onslaught. Their courageous but futile struggle was extinguished with horrifying efficiency. The young men were mown down like so much grain before a mow.

Despite orders from Gutgook to stand their ground and endure the intense battle, the flanks, led by Fokosorot One and Two, retreated in the sixth minute. Gutgook, along with ten brave young warriors, stayed behind until he was shot in the right arm. Unable to use his rifle with his left arm, he was forced to abandon his post and flee.

Gutgook weaved through the maze of huts in the village, dodging gun bullets with each step. Three of Gutgook's brave comrades had already fallen, taken down by expert marksmen. Yet, Gutgook and his remaining seven companions were fortunate enough to escape with their lives, fleeing through the jungle.

The soldiers came to an abrupt halt as the thicket echoed with only the rustling of leaves. The youth's footsteps had faded into an unnatural silence. With heavy hearts, they took up positions in the village, weapons at the ready. In silence, the soldiers stood and watched. Their breath was the only audible sound. Aware that continuing the chase would bring more harm, they decided to settle for guarding the village.

The relentless barrage of bullets had already set multiple huts ablaze, their flames casting a peculiar glow. The soldiers laboured in vain to salvage the burning structures, fighting against the encroaching flames. However, they were met with little success as the fire continued to spread, consuming everything in its path.

As the flames engulfed the village, the soldiers searched for survivors and were able to rescue a few villagers who were trapped in their homes. The soldiers escorted them, determined to protect the innocent from the raging fire. Despite their efforts, the damage was extensive, and many structures were beyond repair.

Amidst the chaos, the soldiers took advantage of the situation, scavenging for anything of value that was left behind. As they rummaged through the scorched ruins, they came across charred goat meat. The soldiers wasted no time feasting on the meat, driven by their hunger and desperation.

The Duomduom village inhabitants who had fled were less fortunate than the feasting soldiers. The community elders were greatly worried about the displaced families and established a small refuge near a water source. The state of the village was rapidly declining, as the military force prevented the inhabitants from returning and thwarted their ability to sustain themselves.

The villagers now had no other option but to rely on the kindness of others. Yet, this was not a sustainable solution. Fortunately, relatives from a nearby cattle ranch came to their rescue, providing them with much-needed nourishment in the form of milk. Despite this generous gesture, it was not enough to fulfil the diverse and urgent needs of the villagers. They lacked vital necessities such as clothing, shelter, and medical supplies.

In the bush where the youths had run for safety, a thick and suffocating regret permeated the atmosphere, a blanket of shared guilt. Silence, heavy and domineering, reigned, punctuated only by the rasping gasps of remorse and the stifled weeping of broken spirits. Their reckless gamble now bore bitter fruit, a stark inversion of their prior arrogance. The shadow of their impulsive act stretched long and menacing, threatening to engulf them. A corrosive remorse ate at their souls, a harsh awakening to the actual cost of their actions. The crushing burden of their collective culpability weighed upon them, a chilling portent of impending retribution. Once envisioned with bright certainty, the future now loomed uncertain and foreboding.

A profound dichotomy of emotion burdened the young people. Some wrestled with the crushing weight of culpability, their ethics and ideals locked in agonising conflict, their inner turmoil a palpable tempest. The repercussions of their choices pressed upon them a suffocating burden of regret. Others, however, stood defiant, their posture rigid, their remorse absent. Their justifications rang with unshakeable certainty, yet a chilling remoteness cloaked them, an unfriendly detachment from the gravity of their acts.

Days of stark isolation in the unforgiving wilderness culminated in a crucial meeting of the village elders. A younger generation, spearheaded by the influential Gutgook, joined their experienced fathers and mothers in the meeting. Following the elders' solemn pronouncement of the meeting's purpose, Gutgook's impassioned voice cut through the silence. He painted a grim picture of rapidly depleting sustenance, his words carrying the weight of impending crisis. The urgency of his plea resonated deeply with me. The previously sceptical youth, their faces now etched with a profound apprehension for their legacy, hung on his every syllable.

Gravity hung heavy in the air as the community's venerable leaders commanded attention. Their faces, etched with the wisdom of countless years, mirrored the precariousness of their shared plight. They recounted a bygone era of harmony and abundance, a golden age in which they implored the younger generation to resurrect through unity. Decorative staffs, emblems of profound knowledge and unwavering authority, rested in their gnarled hands. Each word, laden with the accumulated weight of ancestral experience, was a poignant lament for a lost paradise. A tangible tension, thick with apprehension and anticipation, gripped the assembled youth, their expressions blending yearning and doubt. The elders' fervent appeal struck a chord, a powerful echo of the community's desperate longing for renewal.

The resonating words forged a profound link between the young people and their heritage. A substantial legacy of hardship and devotion, inherited through countless lifetimes, settled upon them. This tangible inheritance instilled a profound sense of duty to their people. Their spirits ignited with a fresh comprehension. Petty divisions must yield to collaborative purpose. A future worthy of their ancestors' sacrifices —a future that would illuminate the path for posterity —became their unwavering objective.

As the discussion progressed, the divide between the two worlds began to blur. The youth realised that they were more similar to their elders than they had previously thought. Gutgook expressed his gratitude for the opportunity to learn from the elders and acknowledged the value of their experience.

Gutgook's sagacious replies astonished the elders. Some thought his perceptions revealed unexpected depths of wisdom. A demonstrable sense of common purpose permeated the atmosphere. The elders breathed a collective sigh of relief, recognising in Gutgook the bourgeoning potential of authentic leadership. This newfound concordance offered a beacon of hope, promising revitalisation to their beleaguered village.

Yet, the solution was not to be found until the army was convinced that those who attacked Nhomlaau town had been arrested. The clan chiefs within the Duomduom communities proposed submitting themselves to the military to facilitate the admission of vulnerable individuals into the village. Despite some resistance from community members, one leader spoke about the responsibility of leadership during both favourable and difficult times. His persuasive words convinced the clan elders.

As they returned to their respective tents, the community members reflected on the day's events. The youth, now armed with the wisdom of their elders, were determined to break down the barriers that had long separated their two worlds.

Chapter Nine

Emerging from their jungle refuge, the Duomduom villagers gazed upon the devastation of their village with stunned horror. The painstaking years of their labour were reduced to smouldering ruins. Their newly constructed homes were incinerated, leaving only ash and the bitter stench of smoke. The livestock—goats and cattle—had perished in the inferno, their charred remains a grim demonstration of the fire's fury. Precious grain stores, their lifeblood, were utterly consumed by the flames.

The devastation caused by the fighting between the youths of Duomduom and the army inflicted wounds far deeper than mere physical destruction. It ravaged irretrievable legacies, obliterating age-old customs and the very soul of their society. Precious artworks were consumed by flames, leaving behind only sterile ash. Once potent magnets drew affluent visitors from Nhomlaau to Duomduom, these drawings and artefacts were irreplaceable conduits of their history and a vital source of economic prosperity through tourism. Their annihilation represented not just a loss of cultural heritage but a devastating blow to their livelihood.

Despair and uncertainty suffocated the village. Villagers, astonished and disoriented, picked through the wreckage of their homes, the catastrophic devastation a stark and horrifying reality. Children's cries pierced the silence, their tiny hands gripping the shaking bodies of their parents. The monumental challenge of materially and emotionally rebuilding weighed upon them an unbearable weight. A fragile spark of hope remained, yet the journey back to normalcy stretched before them, a daunting and perilous journey.

The scale of destruction at Duomduom was undeniable. Any witness to that horrific event would attest to its immensity. A panorama of utter ruin met the gaze. Once a pulsating heart of activity, the village was reduced to a desolate expanse of debris and charred remains. The air, thick with the acrid sting of smoke and the sickening stench of death, hung heavy, a suffocating demonstration of the destruction.

Amidst the wreckage lay the lifeless bodies of men, women, and children, their vacant stares lost in the abyss of eternity. The intricate web of homes, previously teeming with the vibrant energy of a thriving society, now stood as silent, sombre monuments to a brutal onslaught. Each shattered pane, each blackened wall, and each discarded belonging echoed the swift, pitiless violence that had transformed a bustling village into a cemetery of shattered hopes. The survivors carry the permanent, agonising mark of this catastrophic tragedy.

Death permeated the village, its former fragrance of blossoms and freshly baked goods replaced by a sickening stench. Once alive with the pungent perfume of exotic spices, the vibrant marketplace was now a desolate wilderness. War had irrevocably ravaged their idyllic haven. Deserted homes, their windows like hollow sockets, silently bore witness to lives extinguished, their emptiness a stark prophecy of a bleak tomorrow.

A substantial dread, heavier than the dust coating the deserted pathways, settled upon the remaining inhabitants. A mournful wind sighed through the shattered compartments, carrying echoes of joyous exchange and laughter, now supplanted by an oppressive silence. Clinging to each other for solace, the villagers' hope dwindled, a fragile ember threatened by the encroaching darkness. The conflict's wounds were profound, scarring not just the physical landscape but also the souls of the survivors, inflicting trauma that might forever leave them teetering on the precipice of despair.

Amidst the debris, the villagers, their faces imprinted with disbelief, contemplated their future. The catastrophe had not only scattered their possessions but had also crushed the bonds of their tightly woven community. A cloud of devastation hung heavy in the air. The full extent of the destruction was starkly visible. Each footstep was a shuddering encounter with the skeletal remains of their homes, mirroring the fractured state of their lives. The scale of the ruin was utterly crushing, the prospect of restoration seemingly insurmountable.

Rebuilding their shattered village was an extraordinary effort, yet it paled compared to the deeper wounds they carried. After emerging from their forced refuge, their faces bore the grim etchings of profound grief—haunted eyes, devoid of happiness, mirrored spirits fractured by unimaginable suffering. A chilling uncertainty cloaked their future as the villagers wrestled with the overbearing weight of nightmares and searing memories. Once a vibrant flame, hope had been extinguished, leaving only the ashes of despair. The prospect of tomorrow felt bleak, the burden of their losses nearly unbearable.

Crushing despair weighed upon the villagers of Duomduom, every stride a painful reminder of their shared defeat. Internal discord gnawed at their spirits, a grim reflection of the ravaged landscape. Yet, a faint glimmer of hope ignited as some villagers dared to challenge the suffocating power of the repressive gloom, their gazes probing for any break in the impenetrable darkness. A muted dialogue commenced, a hesitant but crucial initial movement towards solidarity. This budding comprehension, though delicate, possessed the power to shatter the walls of their collective blindness. The journey ahead remained shrouded in ambiguity, but the initial seeds of transformation had been planted.

In the aftermath, the surviving villagers faced the enormous task of reconstructing their lives, grappling with the profound loss of their cherished companions. Their mourning was interwoven with the backbreaking labour of resurrecting their once-prosperous settlement from its ashes. A shared agony was their unifying force, creating a precarious bond amidst the devastation. They salvaged what remained, painstakingly reestablishing themselves and nurturing flickering embers of hope, their resolve strengthened by unwavering mutual aid and a collective yearning for stability.

Days bled into weeks, a sombre procession of grief and tireless toil as residents salvaged what scraps of their lives remained. Older people, their features etched with profound sorrow, could only offer heavy-hearted acknowledgement. Their leadership fractured as entirely as the homes they once governed.

A fragile ember of hope flickered against the overwhelming despair. Sharing scant provisions, the villagers clung to each other, their collective spirit a tenacious spark in the encroaching gloom. The arduous task of reconstruction was planned within a matter of days. But it was a slow and agonising climb from the abyss. The agonising search for the missing became the priority, layering further anguish onto the community's already crushing burden. The uncertain horizon stretched before them, a daunting and domineering weight.

Once vibrant with unrestrained glee, the children moved with a subdued stillness, their former innocence shattered by the horrors they'd endured. Laughter, once their constant companion, had been silenced, replaced by the haunting spectre of violence etched onto their young minds. Their innocent eyes, once sparkling with mirth, now reflected a chilling comprehension far exceeding their tender years. Quiet play became a sombre ritual; small, shaking hands meticulously arranging stones, a poignant reflection of their fractured world. A heavy, cruel quietude settled over them, broken only by the occasional hushed murmur, contrasting with their previous excitement. Fear, a constant, gnawing presence, shadowed their gaze. The adults, consumed by their struggle for existence, offered scant comfort, leaving these traumatised youngsters to confront their nightmares alone, a grim and enduring consequence of the conflict's brutal aftermath.

As the days passed, the sound of children's laughter became slowly noticeable. It offered a glimmer of hope in uncertainty. The road ahead was lined with challenges, a demoralising landscape to navigate. Nonetheless, the seeds of determination had been planted, ensuring a steady and determined comeback.

Rebuilding trust between elders and youth seemed impossible. They couldn't return to the peaceful existence they once knew. The emotional wounds inflicted upon them would take longer than the physical ones. The villagers had to muster strength and resilience to move forward, knowing their world would never be the same again. The attack shattered their sense of safety, security, and homes. They would have to adapt to this new, harsh existence, a journey that would be long and arduous.

The results of the miscalculated assault on Nhomlaau ripped through the village's social fabric, leaving a bitter residue of suspicion and animosity. The brutal wounds of internal strife tarnished Duomduom's former sublime charm. A tangible tension replaced its tranquil atmosphere. The previously unified community was splintered, its bonds of fellowship irrevocably broken. A suffocating, miserable apprehension and doubt settled over the village, its future hanging precariously in the balance. The unresolved questions of recompense and vengeance nurtured a volatile instability, threatening to consume what remained.

Overwhelmed by the catastrophic loss of life, the village elders entered a sombre period of self-reflection. Haunted by doubt, they scrutinised their leadership, agonising over their failure to adequately mentor the younger generation. Meanwhile, the formerly defiant youth, confronted with the stark consequences of their rebellion, sank into a heavy silence, their brash spirit utterly broken. A profound shift in communal understanding dawned upon the villagers.

Once overflowing with parental devotion, the villagers now regarded their children with a chilling detachment. Observing their offspring from afar, they saw not the cherished offspring of yesterday but spectral figures adrift in a sea of naivete. The tranquil sanctuary they'd known was shattered; a brutal awakening replaced their blissful ignorance with the stark reality of a world steeped in fear and suspicion. Once a boundless wellspring, parental affection was poisoned by distrust, a bitter legacy of unspeakable violence.

The younger generation, their former radiance dimmed by trauma, mirrored the fractured landscape of their existence. Their once-unblemished spirits, scarred by the horrific event, reflected a world irrevocably corrupted. The villagers' naive belief in a pristine reality had been cruelly shattered, leaving them vulnerable, grappling with the agonising realisation that their idyllic past was permanently extinguished.

The people now eyed each other with suspicion. The years of camaraderie and mutual trust had been eroded by an invisible force that ripped apart their lives. Fear had taken root in their hearts, driving a wedge between them that no logic or reasoning could dislodge. Their once cheery faces now wore the melancholic expressions of those who had lost too much. The distance between neighbours was now palpable. The community was now a shadow of its former self, a mere reflection of the once-happy and harmonious place it had been.

The youth were left to face the harsh reality that their world had been nothing more than a facade. This experience was a valuable lesson for the youth, teaching them the dangers of ignorantly following the authority of another youth. It was a pivotal moment in their journey towards maturity, as they began to understand the power and responsibility that came with knowledge and critical thinking. No longer would they allow themselves to be controlled and deceived by those in positions of power. This realisation ignited a fire within them, turning their fear into anger and their anger into determination to bring about change.

Gutgook's oppressive dominion crumbled. A youthful rebellion, forged in the crucible of tyranny, rose to dismantle his reign. Bound by a shared resolve to escape the pervasive darkness of his misrule, they formed an indomitable alliance. With hearts ablaze and spirits steeled, these courageous young insurgents assaulted the palace, ending Gutgook's brutal hegemony. Their triumph, dearly bought, ushered in an era of precarious peace. The arduous work of reconstruction loomed; the fractured remnants of their society demanded painstaking repair. Undercurrents of discord persisted, a stark reminder that their liberation struggle was only in its nascent stages. The horizon held both the exhilarating potential of a brighter dawn and the chilling presence of unforeseen challenges.

Gutgook's dominion faced a relentless uprising. No longer docile subjects, the young became fervent architects of their destiny. They cast aside naive illusions, recognising a world ripe for transformation, a world where their actions held profound weight, promising a brighter tomorrow for themselves and posterity. This newfound power ignited an unyielding resolve. Their ingenuity manifested in unconventional strategies, constantly outmanoeuvring their tyrannical masters. Amidst the carnage, hope, like a resilient flower, pierced the darkness; anthems of resistance resonated across the devastated landscape, invigorating their spirits. The conflict, though ferocious, forged an indissoluble camaraderie, a demonstration of their bravery that will inspire countless descendants. Their struggle, however, is far from concluded.

Duomduom's young generation, inheriting the wisdom gleaned from their ancestors' trials, navigated the pitfalls of the past with a newfound keenness. They understood the critical need for assertive yet measured dissent, eschewing reckless revolt. Their arduous journey fostered a profound maturity, sharpening their perception of the world's complexities. This transformative growth emboldened them to confront leaders deaf to the guidance of elders, their voices ringing with a compelling blend of respect and righteous challenge.

The villagers were like a fortress, protected from the outside world. But now, the walls had crumbled, leaving them vulnerable to the harsh realities of war. They were divided not just by the conflict but also by their greed, lust for power, and corruption. The war had shattered their peaceful existence. The youth also realised that they were not alone but instead connected to a larger world filled with beauty and chaos.

Daily existence was a brutal struggle for mere survival, a relentless contest against insurmountable odds. Yet, amidst the pervasive hardship, embers of optimism glowed faintly. Though the villagers were physically and emotionally ravaged, their spirits remained unbroken. They stood defiant, their resolve unwavering, nurtured by an unshakeable faith in restoring their tranquil past. The shared memories of a prosperous time past were their bedrock, a constant source of strength. A tenacious hope mirrored in their eyes testified to their indomitable spirit. Even as hunger gnawed and terror stalked them, small acts of compassion provided fleeting reprieves.

However infrequently, the sporadic peals of children's laughter briefly shattered the overbearing gloom. Nonetheless, this tenacious hope faced relentless assaults from impending dangers, pushing them repeatedly to the brink of utter despair. The path ahead remained shrouded in uncertainty, but their perseverance endured.

Indomitable, the villagers' spirits remained unbroken. They were resolutely committed to restoring their ravaged world after enduring profound hardship. A powerful sense of unity emerged from the wreckage of past strife. A fellowship forged in the trial of shared adversity. They were comrades in being. Their collective endeavour focused on reconstruction and recovery. Their resilience, tempered by unrelenting trials, blazed forth. Communal feasts and the sharing of narratives cemented their bonds. Hope, a persistent spark defying the encompassing gloom, ignited by their solid determination, flickered to life. Ancient wisdom, imparted by the village elders, illuminated the path for the younger generation, guiding them toward a radiant future, a future they would collaboratively create.

Amid their collective striving for a brighter tomorrow, the villagers found refuge in shared experiences. Their mutual confidences, a tapestry woven with hardship and heartache, yielded unexpected solace. The knowledge of their interconnected struggles forged an indomitable spirit, binding them with unshakeable resolve. Each narrative of perseverance ignited a beacon of hope, its glow intensifying with every recounted triumph. Once a scarce commodity, joy now resonated through the village heart, vibrant evidence of their newfound solidarity. The children, revitalised, leapt with unrestrained cheerfulness.

However, the road ahead remained ambiguous. Foreboding shadows persisted, yet their collective strength faced them without flinching. The villagers understood their arduous journey was only beginning.

Overcoming their discord, the villagers of Duomduom village collaborated, not merely restoring a portion of their village but forging a resilient community from the ashes. Shared toil unexpectedly blossomed into profound friendships, dissolving longstanding animosities. Unforeseen bonds, stronger than they'd ever envisioned, emerged from the storehouse of their collective effort. This spirit of unity transcended mere reconstruction; it permeated their existence, replacing ancient enmities with a powerful sense of shared purpose. Their revitalised community, saturated with renewed vigour and optimism, now confronted the future with unwavering determination, prepared to conquer any obstacle.

Gutgook and his companions lived through long, lonely stretches, increasingly alienated from the younger generation they had once guided. Time, relentlessly marching onward, gradually acclimates them to their altered circumstances. They witnessed, with a growing sense of detachment, the shift in allegiance as the youth sought wisdom from other sources. A profound rift emerged, a stark separation between established traditions and the burgeoning innovations of the new age.

The once-avid pupils, now pursuing divergent trajectories, left the elders in a secluded world of their own. Initially disheartened by this rejection, the elders, surprisingly, discovered a peculiar tranquillity in their quiet contemplation. They became astute observers, discerning valuable lessons from the evolving landscape. Yet, this serene reflection was frequently interrupted by gnawing anxieties. Would the untested choices of the young ultimately lead to ruin? The uncertainty of the future cast a long shadow.

Following the incineration of Duomduom, the occupying forces abruptly withdrew upon the villagers' courageous return. Their unexpected departure, a beacon in the oppressive darkness of conflict, confirmed the villagers' precarious safety. This retreat felt like a divine intervention, a sunburst piercing the war's brutal storm clouds. Hope, previously a flickering ember, blazed brightly within the hearts of the Duomduom people. The army's absence provided the much-needed sanctuary, an unshakable safeguard against further devastation. The resilient village prepared for a triumphant resurgence from the ashes of destruction.

The army's departure was not a mere withdrawal. Having fulfilled their obligation of defence by defeating the youth of Duomduom, they had also apprehended the village's authority figures. The chiefs and elders, now incarcerated in the proximate town of Nhomlaau, awaited trial for the offences of their impetuous youth.

After the army had left, the village was once again at peace, and the villagers were grateful to their leaders, who had surrendered themselves to the military to save their people from further harm. The leaders had been imprisoned and tortured, but had managed to prevent further destruction. Only through their relentless efforts, as they kept talking to Nhomlaau authorities while in prison, did the army finally agree to vacate the area and leave the villagers. This act of selflessness had truly touched their hearts.

For Gutgook and his companions, this was only the beginning of their trouble. The atrocities they had committed while in power were exposed, and they were going to be held accountable for their actions. The weight of their deeds began to burden them as they realised that their once noble intentions had been corrupted by the power bestowed upon them by their peers. While the villagers prospered and rebuilt, Gutgook and his comrades faced the consequences of their choices. They had become victims of their own ignorance, and the cloud of authority that had blinded them had finally been lifted.

Chapter Ten

Several weeks after the military withdrew from Nhomlaau town, the imprisoned leaders of Duomduom village were summoned before Judge Solomon Brown. The leaders numbered thirteen. Upon arrival at the courthouse in a prison vehicle, they were led into the judge's chamber. The leaders were visibly nervous as they stood before the judge.

The judge's chamber was large, and the walls were lined with shelves of old books and legal documents. The room was brightly lit, and the smell of musty paper and ink lingered. It was evident that this chamber held great importance. The long wooden table in front of the leaders of Duomduom seemed to stretch on forever.

Judge Brown, a man of unwavering severity yet impartial judgment, noted their unmistakable anxiety. His throat clearing resounded, a stark punctuation in the tense quiet that only heightened their discomfort. The thirteen chiefs, each a potent symbol of the Duomduom's fractured power structure, traded furtive, apprehensive looks. Their destinies teetered on the knife's edge.

The looming spectre of harsh penalties—a grim echo of the recent bloodshed—weighed heavily on their souls. The proceedings had commenced, and the gravity of their situation was undeniable.

The judge's prominence was a chilling prelude. Known for his uncompromising adherence to the letter of the law, he brooked no leniency within his chambers. A chilly stare, sweeping the hushed courtroom, quelled even the faintest murmur. Justice, for him, was an unyielding, monolithic force. His judgments, definitive and irreversible, shaped countless destinies. But beneath this façade of unbending severity, a quiet reflection glowed—a subtle questioning, perhaps, or the substantial weight of his unwavering rectitude.

The impending trial consumed Judge Brown's attention utterly. Even when the hearing hadn't commenced, a profound sense of responsibility weighed upon him. He understood the stark disparity: the chiefs, defenceless against the formidable legal arsenal wielded by the affluent townspeople's expensive counsel, required his meticulous scrutiny.

The Duomduom community leaders were accused of inciting violence against the neighbouring community of Nhomlaau. The judge's recitation of the charges elicited a profound sense of despair. Yet, a firm conviction in the impartiality of the legal process and a steadfast belief in the eventual triumph of truth sustained their spirits.

The esteemed elders of Duomduom, figures deeply respected within their community, were aghast at the brutal allegations levelled against them. Many townsfolk, familiar with the chiefs' longstanding reputation for tranquillity, found the accusations incredible. Yet, the Nhomlaau people presented compelling evidence – seemingly incontrovertible eyewitness testimonies detailing the horrific violence perpetrated by Duomduom's youth.

The courtroom was thick with the suffocating weight of these damning claims.

"I believe," Judge Brown began, "you have understood the charges against you very well. I want to hear your responses to these charges."

Duomduom's Executive Chief sat erect, his bearing reflecting an erudite and tranquil mind. His pronouncements in the customary tribunal were the bedrock of his colleagues' decisions; their reliance on his wisdom was absolute. Now, they sought his brilliance, his initial response to the magistrate, to avoid a needless quagmire of legal complexities.

"We have understood the charges, my lord," said the Executive Chief. "However, we are here as leaders of Duomduom to accuse Mr. Loi, the town's banker. He had been conspiring with local business people who hired others to sneak into the pastures of Duomduom and illegally milk cows in the wilderness. The milk was then sold in town, leaving the community impoverished and in despair. The children, who depended on the milk from the cows, were the most affected during this difficult time."

A stunned silence descended upon the courtroom, replaced only by the rustling murmur of disbelief. Mr. Loi, a man whose impeccable standing had always preceded him, was now the subject of an astonishing accusation. The community's unwavering esteem crumbled under the weight of this unexpected indictment. Their former admiration now felt naive, tainted by uncertainty. This revelation prompted a profound reassessment of their long-held beliefs, sparking a passionate desire for a thorough investigation. Nevertheless, no one uttered a word.

"Gutgook and other youth leaders had warned Mr. Loi and the businessmen," continued the Executive Chief, "but their pleas had fallen on deaf ears. The youth of Duomduom community had no choice, despite the chiefs' and elders' advice to solve the problem differently, but to take matters into their own hands and retaliate against the banker."

The unexpected disclosure stunned the magistrate. His gaze sharpened, fixing on the courtroom bailiff. "Retrieve Mr. Loi immediately and bring him to the court to defend himself," the judge barked the orders. With a curt command, the bailiff dispatched a group of officers. The selected law enforcement contingent responded with practised efficiency. They went to the bank swiftly, apprehending the affluent financier and transporting him, without delay, to the courtroom while the judge was still waiting. The attendees of the court hearing were also waiting inside the courtroom.

As Mr. Loi stepped into the courtroom, a tangible tension hung in the air. A man who had always been revered in their community was now facing a grave accusation. The judge couldn't believe it. How could someone like Mr. Loi, who had always been kind and generous, be accused of such a heinous crime? He had known Mr. Loi for years and couldn't help but feel torn between his relationship with the accused and his duty as a judge. He knew his decision after the hearing would significantly impact Mr. Loi and the Duomduom community.

Mr. Loi looked around the courtroom and noticed the curious gazes of the onlookers. He could feel the judgmental eyes of those around him. He knew the matter at hand pertained to the recent attack on his lavish estate, but he couldn't fathom why the judge seemed displeased with him. He was an innocent victim of an unprovoked assault on his family.

The judge's voice boomed across the room, breaking the silence. "Mr. Loi, you have been called here today to face the charges brought against you for the recent attack on your estate.

The evidence against you is strong, and I hope you have a strong defence."

As Mr. Loi stood before the judge, he could feel the weight of the man's gaze bearing down on him. The judge's expression was stern, and it was clear that excuses would not sway him. Mr. Loi searched his mind for any possible defence but couldn't find anything strong enough. The judge stared at him as if he were trying to see through to the man's soul.

"I am ready to hear what I am accused of, my lord," Mr. Loi broke the silence.

The bright lights illuminated every detail, from the sweat on Mr. Loi's forehead to the wrinkles on the judge's brow. Mr. Loi's hands trembled. He couldn't help but feel a sense of betrayal from the judge, someone he had always looked up to and respected. As he stood there, he knew he had to trust in the justice system. He knew he was innocent, and he was determined to prove it. Yet, he couldn't help but feel like he was fighting a losing battle.

Judge Brown, his voice heavy with the weight of the accusations, addressed the defendant. "The Executive Chief of Duomduom, representing his people in this solemn proceeding, alleges that you perpetrated a sustained theft of their livestock's milk. Despite repeated admonishments, your actions remained unrepentant. This egregious and persistent pilfering ignited the fury of the Duomduom youth, provoking a violent assault upon your property, resulting in a tragic and regrettable loss of life on both sides of this horrific conflict."

"My lord, the Judge," Mr. Loi began. "I do not understand how I could be accused of the crime directed against me. I have not committed any crime that resulted in the attack on my family. I consider myself innocent."

The judge's dark robes, brilliantly adorned with intricate golden trim, seemed to swallow Mr. Loi. The courtroom walls closed in, and he felt suffocated, drowning in condemnation. This starkly contrasted to the calm, cool demeanour of the judge, who sat stoically behind his imposing desk. His expression was unreadable. Even amidst the tension and uncertainty, Mr. Loi couldn't help but feel a sense of awe towards the judge. His mere presence commanded respect and obedience, and Mr. Loi couldn't help but wonder about the life this man must lead.

The courtroom was packed with curious onlookers, all waiting to see how the trial would end. Many had already decided about Mr. Loi, convinced of his guilt. Others were more sympathetic, giving him the benefit of the doubt. Mr. Loi could feel the eyes of the courtroom on him, judging him, accusing him. The cold wooden bench beneath him was a sharp reminder of his vulnerability. He longed to reach out and grasp the comforting warmth of his family's hands, but they were not there.

"Did you say you are innocent, Mr. Loi?" asked the judge, leaning forward in his chair.

"Yes, my lord," Mr. Loi responded without hesitation. "I am innocent and would like my accuser to prove me guilty."

"Can any of you, chiefs, produce the evidence that Mr. Loi has been involved in milking your cows in the wilderness?" asked the judge.

As the chiefs of Duomduom village exchanged glances, the Executive Chief called the translator to come closer and began to speak in his mother tongue. The translator's heart raced as he approached the Executive Chief, hoping to accurately translate the words that were about to be spoken. He understood the significance of his role in these court proceedings, as it would ultimately determine the future of his people. He stood before the chief and took a deep breath, listening to the words spoken in his native tongue.

The Executive Chief also felt profound anxiety. He feared a single misinterpretation of his words could fatally undermine their argument. He posed a critical test to gauge the interpreter's proficiency: asking him to translate a key passage from their native language, written document, into English, the judge's native tongue. The interpreter translated it well. His confidence alleviated the Chief's anxiety but did not entirely dispel his apprehension.

"Your Honour," began the Executive Chief of Duomduom, "I can be forthright in stating that those aware of Mr. Loi's transgression are our youth leaders. Our imprisonment is not due to possessing information on the banker's case. Instead, we subjected ourselves to confinement to persuade our people to return to their humble village homes. I respectfully request the presence of three youth leaders, Gutgook, Fokosorot One, and Fokosorot Two, to testify to the exact actions of the banker. As someone who presides over trials, I understand the gravity of giving testimony in a court of law."

The translator accurately translated every word uttered by the Executive Chief. He could feel the weight of his words and their impact on both worlds as he spoke English. With every sentence, he chose his words and conveyed the true meaning of the Executive Chief's message. This was a delicate dance between two worlds, and he was determined to bridge the gap.

"Thank you for this suggestion, Chief," said the judge. "I adjourn the court for two hours so that we can wait for the suggested youth leaders to come. I want one of you, the chiefs, to go and bring these youth leaders. Sending the police to the village would lead to chaos since the attack by the army on the village less than a month ago is still fresh on the minds of the people. I want the car that often takes the medical doctor to Duomduom to be the one that takes those of you who will volunteer to go."

The Executive Chief and his assistant offered to embark on the journey to Duomduom. The judge was greatly impressed by their courage and unfaltering commitment and deemed them the most suitable individuals for the task. He instructed the driver to transport the chiefs to Duomduom village and bring them back to the court chambers in Nhomlaau town.

The driver had been trained to be obedient and respectful. Therefore, he thought it was not his role to question the magistrate's orders. After all, he had been working at the hospital for many years and had never encountered any issues with how things were run. As he drove towards Duomduom, he felt uneasy about the fate of the youth leaders. He wondered if they were guilty or mere victims of false accusations.

Witnessing firsthand the young leaders' fervent devotion to their community's betterment – a dedication manifested in their tireless service to at-risk youth – left the driver profoundly unsettled by the accusations they levelled against the banker. The allegations, preposterous in their severity, gnawed at his conscience. He feared the potential repercussions for these selfless individuals, whose tireless work was a powerful testament to their integrity and dedication. This blatant injustice, this outrage, ignited a fierce resolve within him.

During their transit from Nhomlaau to Duomduom, the Executive Chief and his entourage comprehensively answered the driver's inquisitive queries. Intensely interested in the Chief's impending trial, the driver persistently probed for specifics concerning the contentious issues between the youth and Mr. Loi. He gleaned a fragile possibility of an amicable settlement, centred on discussions around equitable restitution and collaborative resource management. This offered a faint ray of optimism, yet underlying scepticism between the disputants persisted, casting a long shadow of doubt.

Upon arrival at Duomduom, the Executive Chief and his assistant received a warm reception from a crowd anxious about their well-being during prison. The Executive Chief wasted no time and announced that the court proceedings had commenced, and Gutgook, Fokosorot One, and Fokosorot Two were summoned to testify.

The news evoked a mixture of excitement and trepidation. The youth leaders were eager, but also feared the consequences of speaking out against an influential figure in town. The elders, who were related to the youth leaders, gathered their belongings and prepared to accompany them to court. They knew their presence would provide support to the courageous youth. With resolute, unwavering solidarity, the group promptly embarked on their journey back to Nhomlaau town.

A significant delay ensued before the Duomduom villagers finally entered the hushed chamber, their tardiness stretching the proceedings by ninety minutes. The Executive Chief, with immediate dispatch, apprised the judge of their presence, prompting a resumption of the hearing. Their dramatic entrance ignited a buzz; silent murmurs swept through the charged atmosphere. A pregnant silence followed.

As the judge took his seat and gazed over the courtroom, he could see the stark contrast between the two worlds in his courtroom. On one side were the privileged, well-dressed individuals who held power and influence. On the other hand, the poor and marginalised were represented by the group that had just arrived.

"Are the youth leaders from Duomduom here?" The judge asked, and the youth leaders affirmed their presence by showing their hands.

"Delighted to have you here," the judge remarked. "Please enlighten me on your knowledge regarding Mr. Loi's involvement in the purported mistreatment of your community." The translator put the question as precisely as the judge had asked it in English.

Addressing the esteemed judge, Gutgook, the youth leader of Duomduom, commenced his testimony. He, the architect of the brutal assault on the banker's luxurious estate, an attack that tragically claimed innocent lives in Nhomlaau, stood resolute. "My confession, my lord, concerns Mr. Loi's treacherous scheme. He secretly financed the systematic plunder of milk from our cattle, the illicit sale of which enriched him in the Nhomlaau marketplace. Despite our impassioned pleas and warnings to the milk thieves, our words were brushed aside. Driven to desperation by this protracted and obvious disregard, we launched our retaliatory strike against Mr. Loi's residence. While we deeply lament the accidental deaths of bystanders—individuals unconnected to this dairy theft—we hold Mr. Loi solely accountable for these horrific events."

Each one of the three youth leaders in the court droned on about rumours of the banker's shady dealings. The judge's attention masked his mounting frustration, his eyes darting back and forth between the speaker and the evidence.

As the final youth leader fell silent, the judge sat up straight in his chair and fixed his gaze upon the trio of young leaders. He then inquired, "Have you personally observed everything you have relayed, or have others informed you?"

"Other people told us," Gutgook chimed in.

"And you believed them?" asked the judge.

"Yes," responded Gutgook. "We believed them."

"Who are these people?" asked the judge. "Can you name them so that we summon them here in this court?"

"We cannot remember exactly who they were," responded Fokosorot Two, "but we remember that they told us what we have narrated here."

"Is that the best answer the rest of you can give?" asked the judge.

Gutgook and Fokosorot One nodded in agreement.

"Say it so that I know it is your true answer to my question," demanded the judge.

"We confirm it is our answer," replied Gutgook and Fokosorot One almost in unison.

As the youth leaders delivered their final response, the judge reclined against his chair, maintaining silence. It dawned on him that the youth of Duomduom may have acted hastily in their pursuit of justice. Their limited understanding and knowledge of the situation may have prompted impulsive decisions. Their perspective may have been altered if they had taken the time to comprehend the complexities.

The ignorance shrouding the Duomduom youth's minds prevented them from seeing the whole picture. However, it was also essential to consider that the villagers acted out of desperation and a deep-seated need for justice. Thus, while their actions may have been misguided, they were driven by a genuine desire for fairness and equality.

The judge stood up and rested his hands on the table, his black robe billowing around him as he rose from his chair. With a commanding voice, he declared that the trial would be adjourned until the following day. Everyone knew that the judge's ruling would have a profound impact on the case's outcome. As he sat back down, the judge's expression remained unreadable.

A surge of people spilt from the courthouse, a cacophony of voices mingling with the rhythmic thud of countless feet. The descending sun painted the vibrant street in hues of amber as the throng retreated to their dwellings in Nhomlaau, a town now heavy with unspoken tension. Meanwhile, the chiefs and youth leaders, their countenances grim with apprehension, were herded into a waiting prison van. With the vehicle's departure, the crowd dissipated, leaving behind a deep sense of dread. The protracted night that followed would be measured in the chilling silence of their confinement, their destinies hanging precariously in the balance.

As the sun rose the following day, the courtroom bustled again with activity. The judge's designated time had arrived, and a crowd of individuals had gathered. Gutgook and the two other young leaders came together with the chiefs of Duomduom in the prison van and entered the courtroom silently. They stood in the centre of the courtroom, surrounded by their anxious supporters. They knew that the judge's conclusion of the case would not be in their favour.

Silence descended, a substantial weight settling upon the courtroom as a commanding presence filled the doorway. The atmosphere crackled with the unspoken gravity of the impending judgment. The judge's glacial gaze, sharp and unforgiving, spoke volumes about the solemn proceedings to follow. A collective intake of breath, a hushed anticipation, hung in the air. Nervous tremors vibrated through the assembled onlookers; even the most experienced legal minds felt the suffocating intensity. The moment of reckoning had arrived.

The judge began recounting the various arguments that both sides had made. His voice echoed through the courtroom, each word carrying immense weight. The audience held their breath, anxiously waiting for the verdict.

The judge's pronouncement concluded, the falling gavel a stark punctuation to the weighty decree. A suffocating stillness descended, punctuated only by the ragged gasps of those present. Euphoria flooded one faction; the other, drowning in bleak resignation. Yet, a profound sense of incompleteness lingered; the verdict, for many, felt far from definitive. Anticipated appeals foreshadowed a protracted legal war, the conflict's resolution remaining frustratingly distant.

Gutgook, the main accused, was sentenced to a lifetime behind bars for his crimes. Fokosorot One and Fokosorot Two, his accomplices, were imprisoned for twenty years. The banker had been declared innocent. The chiefs were also implicated and were acquitted and released from custody. Some hung their heads in defeat, while others cried joy and relief. The judge's verdict had divided the two worlds in the courtroom, each side holding onto their own version of justice.

Chapter Eleven

An overwhelming awareness of their fortunate circumstances descended upon the people of Nhomlaau, shattering their complacency. The glaring inequalities within their community became inescapably apparent, stirring deep unease. As the veil of obliviousness lifted, they were confronted with the stark dichotomy between their lives and the abject hardship endured by their neighbours. The suffering surrounding them became a searing revelation, a painful truth they could no longer avoid. The harsh realities, previously unseen, now pressed upon them with insistent force, demanding attention. This uncomfortable confrontation compelled the residents of Nhomlaau to critically examine the inherent injustices of their society, a process fraught with unsettling self-reflection.

Even though Judge Brown ruled differently, Nhomlaau's citizens, accustomed to lives of extravagant ease, believed they faced a shattering revelation: their prosperity was founded on the misery of others. The merciless exploitation of the Duomduom people by wealthy business people, who amassed colossal fortunes through pitiless automated milking, became shockingly clear. A profound ethical dilemma gripped them. The inescapable weight of their unwitting complicity in this oppressive dealing crushed the inhabitants of Nhomlaau, leaving them burdened by guilt and pierced by a newfound empathy for the wretched Duomduom.

The appalling discovery, however, unexpectedly kindled a solid determination within them. A deep self-examination led to a solemn pledge: to cultivate a robust and equitable alliance with Duomduom, built on genuine empathy and a commitment to restorative justice. This transformative encounter became the crucible in which Nhomlaau's radical reformation was forged, a stimulus for enduring and meaningful societal renewal.

The citizens of Nhomlaau wrestled with the complex implications of their newfound circumstances, recognising the daunting obstacles that loomed. The actual perpetrators of injustice were finally exposed, revealing the potent force inherent in their collective resolve – a unified commitment to securing a brighter future for themselves and their Duomduom neighbours. Their deeply held faith in the Almighty Creator, the architect of all existence, fuelled their conviction. This God, they believed, witnessed every clandestine deed, rendering any complicity in the oppression of the vulnerable Duomduom people an unforgivable transgression, punishable by divine retribution if the people of Nhomlaau remained passive in the face of such suffering.

Deep disappointment consumed the Nhomlaau elders. The town's administration, they painfully acknowledged, was crippled by incompetence. Months of festering resentment between Nhomlaau and the neighbouring Duomduom culminated in a savage attack on Nhomlaau by Duomduom youths. This attack triggered a ferocious military counter-strike against the

Duomduom settlement. A deep sense of regret permeated their thoughts. They believed that preventative measures should have been put in place to prevent the attacks. They were now firmly committed to systemic reform within the town's management.

A succession of elders voiced identical sentiments during discussions, their weighty pronouncements culminating in a singular resolution: dispatching a representative to the Duomduom leadership. This envoy would convey a heartfelt contrition for the transgressions committed by a small fraction of misguided Nhomlaau residents. The council acknowledged the conflict stemmed not from widespread animosity, but from the reckless machinations of a few greedy businessmen. Despite pervasive anxieties, the elders resolved to rectify the situation with unwavering resolve.

Following a meeting with Nhomlaau's mayor, the town's elders advocated for a formal letter of contrition to Duomduom. This act of remorse, they asserted, would unequivocally demonstrate Nhomlaau's acknowledgement of the egregious offence against its neighbour. Although the perpetrator, who was pilfering milk from Duomduom's cattle, remained elusive, the elders acknowledged the undeniable link between the youth's assault on Nhomlaau and the subsequent quick decline in milk supplies at the Nhomlaau market. The mayor readily consented to compose the apology, representing the collective guilt of Nhomlaau's citizenry.

With the olive branch extended and the fate of both communities hanging in the balance, the elders were hopeful that the Duomduom chiefs would accept the apology from the people of Nhomlaau town and agree to have a peaceful coexistence between their two sisterly communities. They knew that whatever the outcome of the apology would be, it would have a lasting impact on the future of both communities.

The mayor of Nhomlaau town had been elected to lead his people because of his reputation for fairness and sound decision-making. He had worked tirelessly to ensure that the people of Nhomlaau could live in peace and prosperity, and had always been a staunch supporter of maintaining good relations with neighbouring communities.

The mayor's love for harmonious living among communities drove him to listen to the concerns of Nhomlaau's elders. They expressed their worries about the strained ties with Duomduom, and the mayor knew their concerns were valid. He understood the significance of maintaining a delicate balance between the two communities, as it was crucial for the area's stability. Nhomlaau and Duomduom shared a deep-rooted cultural and ethnic connection, and any rift between them could have severe consequences.

After much thought and consideration, the mayor heeded the counsel of the elders and composed a letter of remorse, apologising for the actions of the townsfolk. With the letter in hand, the mayor prepared it for dispatch to Duomduom. He knew it was a small step, but he believed it was a step in the right direction toward building a better future for both Nhomlaau and Duomduom.

A delegation, led by the village's beloved physician, Dr. Jameson, journeyed to Duomduom, carrying the apology letter. Years of battling malaria had cemented his standing within the community, even amidst the bitter feud that had erupted between Duomduom and Nhomlaau. The weight of the mayor's desperate plea for forgiveness rested heavily upon his shoulders, a stark contrast to his usual composure. He, a pillar of tranquillity in the turbulence of conflict, represented the Nhomlaau community's fervent yearning for peace. Decades of unwavering service had cultivated an unbreakable link of trust between Nhomlaau and

Duomduom. Citizens of Nhomlaau had been financially supporting Dr. Jameson's work.

Flanking him were three esteemed elders of Nhomlaau, their countenances reflecting both apprehension and fervent hope, a potent symbol of their faith in his mediating skills. Their collective prayer for an end to the bloodshed and the antagonism that resulted from the fighting resonated deeply. This small but powerfully symbolic group, guided by a revered figurehead, embarked on this vital mission, their resolve unshaken by the looming uncertainty.

Dr. Jameson's vehicle, a comforting presence in the twin communities of Nhomlaau and Duomduom, had become an emblem of their collective happiness. Its approach invariably ignited expectations of solace and security. The unwavering faith the villagers placed in the doctor profoundly enhanced the car's positive aura. This implicit trust served as a powerful adhesive, binding Nhomlaau and Duomduom in a shared sense of community. Yet, this particular trip carried a palpable undercurrent of apprehension; an unsettling premonition overshadowed the car's normally auspicious arrival.

During their journey to Duomduom, Dr. Jameson's curiosity was piqued regarding the genesis of the mayor's conciliatory gesture. His three elderly companions, acting as emissaries of wisdom, meticulously recounted the events. In a solemn gathering within Nhomlaau's council of elders, a momentous decision was reached: a formal apology, a balm for the fractured harmony between their town and the villagers of Duomduom, was deemed the most efficacious path to reconciliation. This resolution was subsequently conveyed to the mayor, who, embracing the proposal with fervent enthusiasm, immediately composed the letter of amends.

The physician lauded the mayor's courageous initiatives, predicting enthusiastic widespread acclaim throughout Duomduom. Citizens, yearning to mend the fractured ties with their neighbours, desperately needed this beacon of hope amidst the turbulent chapter of their past. This bold action laid the groundwork for a transformative era, one characterised by a collaborative spirit and mutual comprehension, where disagreements would yield to respectful discourse and compromise.

Just as the doctor was about to elaborate, a vehicle materialised at Duomduom's edge, a joyous chorus erupted as the children, their faces alight with anticipation, sprinted towards the approaching car, their cries of "Welcome, Doctor! We've longed for your return!" echoing through the air. Through the car's window, the physician acknowledged their enthusiastic greeting with a warm wave. The children, their excitement unmistakable, flanked the vehicle, a vibrant escort leading it to their customary rendezvous beneath the village's majestic central tree. The Nhomlaau watched the children running on both sides of the vehicle but said nothing.

Long before the doctor's Land Cruiser, a veteran vehicle wheezing clouds of dust, sputtered into the village square, the residents of Duomduom had assembled beneath the shade of the ancient tamarind tree. A tangible thrum of anticipation vibrated through the crowd. They yearned to hear the pronouncements of Dr. Jameson, whose prolonged absence had stoked both concern and fervent hope. His commitment to their well-being was legendary, his tireless efforts on their behalf a cherished memory.

As Dr. Jameson emerged from the vehicle, flanked by esteemed Nhomlaau elders, a profound silence descended on the crowd. The weight of their collective anxieties and aspirations seemed to press down on his heavy medical bag. The villagers instinctively knew this consultation would be protracted and momentous. Dr.

Jameson never wasted time. He moved with the delegation to the front section of the meeting and took his seat. Anxious elders of Nhomlaau, hastily seated near the physician, fidgeted in their chairs.

Dr. Jameson's tranquil composure stood in stark contrast to the elders' grim faces, etched with worry. Their hushed murmurs, barely audible beneath the expansive branches, spoke volumes of their plight. He commenced his address, measured and deliberate, each word carrying significant weight. The translator, however, laboured to maintain the pace, his voice taut with the urgency of the message.

A profound stillness, thick with anticipation, descended upon the gathering. Yet, beneath this tense calm, a palpable unrest vibrated through the swelling throng—a volatile blend of dread and fervent longing that pulsed with every carefully chosen word from Dr. Jameson. He paused, his gaze keenly assessing their responses.

Eventually, Dr. Jameson extended his hand, accepting the mayoral missive from a respected elder of Nhomlaau. As he perused the document, the interpreter's voice, a counterpoint to the rustling pages, provided a simultaneous translation. A profound hush gripped the assembly; not a soul so much as batted away a bothersome insect. Upon completing the letter, a wave of tumultuous acclaim washed over the physician, then subsided as swiftly as it began, leaving behind an echoing stillness.

With heavy hearts, the three venerable leaders commenced their address. Profuse apologies, issued on behalf of the Nhomlaau populace, resonated with genuine contrition. Their eloquent plea highlighted the enduring legacy of shared experiences—a kinship far outweighing the bitterness of recent strife. A solemn commitment to renewed collaboration, to mend fractured alliances, flowed from their lips. A profound wave of feeling washed over the gathering; reconciliation hung tangible in the air. The fragile seed of a united tomorrow sprouted, promising a future of harmony. This nascent unity, however precarious, demanded diligent cultivation. The journey forward required steady communication and mutual respect.

During the talks, the youth of Duomduom understood the importance of mending what had been broken. They wholeheartedly embraced the idea of working together with community leaders to bridge the gap and revive the lost trust and bond between Nhomlaau and Duomduom. They found a new sense of purpose, which was to reunite the two worlds that were once connected. As they listened more carefully to the speeches of the elders of Nhomlaau, the youth of Duomduom realised that the animosity between the two communities had slowly dissipated. They understood that the younger generation would play a crucial role in this change, even if they were not the ones who took the first step towards reconciliation.

With their fresh outlook and unwavering resolve, the youth resolved to reconcile the long-lost balance and solidarity between the two sisterly communities. Their steps forward would not be easy, as the shadows of the past haunted them, but with a renewed sense of optimism and faith, they would push through the barriers and emerge as victors over the cloud of ignorance. The tale of the two worlds would forever serve as a demonstration of the power of reconciliation. It would serve as a reminder that, no matter how deep the divide may seem, there is always a chance to bridge the gap and find common ground.

Some elders in Duomduom, however, were resistant to the idea of forgiveness, especially when it came to the actions of their youth under the rule of Gutgook. There was a fear that if they were to forgive the youth and forget, it would encourage further acts of insubordination from the younger generation. They had worked hard to maintain their power and control in their world and were not willing to risk losing it to a group of rebellious youths.

The intractable animosity between some elders of Duomduom and their youth finally yielded to the persuasive wisdom of the elders present in the meeting. Nhomlaau's leaders skilfully argued that extending a pardon to their community implicitly forgave all involved. Why, then, would Duomduom elders withhold clemency from their offspring? This compelling logic resonated deeply. The Duomduom elders, initially steadfast in their refusal to pardon the youth, were ultimately moved by the unifying potential of collective amnesty. This momentous decision, heralded as a pivotal breakthrough, marked the end of a bitter chapter spanning generations.

A substantial sense of relief replaced the suffocating weight of longstanding resentment. Hope, fragile yet potent, sprouted amidst the ruins of months of conflict. This nascent unity, however, represented merely a tentative first step. The daunting challenge of rebuilding fractured trust and forging enduring peace loomed large, signalling a future of complex negotiations—a journey filled with both extraordinary possibilities and inherent risks.

After the emotions had subsided between some elders of Duomduom and their youth, the doctor stood up and revealed that the judge, who had initially sentenced Gutgook to a lifetime of hard labour, had reconsidered his ruling because the Nhomlaau residents had come forward with a confession, admitting local business owners were involved in the exploitation of Duomduom's cows. This new information had a significant impact on the judge's decision, and he decided to lessen the punishment for the three young leaders to a mere three-year term each. The people in the meeting erupted in applause, grateful for the change in ruling.

Duomduom people had never expected this outcome, having lived for so long in a state of hostility and conflict. It was a moment of revelation for all, as they realised that their aggression and retaliation had only brought them pain and suffering.

The doctor requested the Duomduom's Executive Chief's presence to accompany him so that the mayor could fully comprehend that the inhabitants of Duomduom had accepted his apology. The community and the Executive Chief embraced the doctor's plea, and together, they set off towards the town of Nhomlaau. They arrived in town and proceeded directly to the mayor's office to meet and brief him on the mission he had assigned to them.

The physician's appearance at the office brought word to the mayor of Nhomlaau town that the Duomduom populace had not merely accepted the apology from Nhomlaau's people, but also exhibited heartfelt contrition for their brutal attack. Initially dubious, a profound sense of liberation swept over the mayor. He had anticipated arduous, protracted talks. This unforeseen concordance paved the way for a future partnership between Nhomlaau and Duomduom, ushering in an unprecedented era of tranquillity. Subsequent dialogues were scheduled to address fundamental grievances and pre-empt future hostilities.

The town mayor was relieved to see that there was a chance for reconciliation. He urged the Executive Chief of Duomduom to return to Duomduom and bring the chiefs and elders of the village to commemorate the reconciliation between the two communities. The Executive Chief agreed. The doctor gave him the vehicle to take him back to Duomduom.

The following day, the inhabitants of Duomduom made their way to the town of Nhomlaau to partake in the celebrations. The streets were lined with colourful decorations, and the sound of joyful music filled the air. Children ran around playing games, while adults greeted each other with hugs and laughter. The whole town was buzzing with excitement and anticipation.

With the sun dipping below the horizon, the mayor, silhouetted against the fiery sky, commanded the town square's attention. His voice, a powerful current amplified by a sputtering microphone, surged through the assembled throng, a proclamation of harmony and advancement. He articulated a vision of shared prosperity and synergistic endeavours. A collective breath was held as he revealed blueprints for a vibrant community centre, a beacon illuminating their newly forged unity. Children's laughter mingled with the expectant smiles of their guardians.

The fading light painted the square in breathtaking shades of amber and violet, foreshadowing a promising tomorrow. The path ahead stretched long, yet the inaugural stride had been made. Citizens from both communities, their faces alight with optimism, hung on his every word, their hearts brimming with the anticipation of a brighter era. This pivotal moment, etched in the annals of their collective memory, would resonate through countless generations to come.

The people of Nhomlaau and Duomduom had learned from their past mistakes and were now committed to building a better future together. As they moved forward, they knew that they could count on each other for support and strength. The town and village communities had truly come a long way, and their newfound unity was a demonstration of the power of forgiveness and understanding. The physician's dedicated service to the community had not only brought physical healing but also emotional healing, bridging the gap between the two worlds and paving the way for a brighter future.

The Duomduom Executive Chief's newfound view of the people of Nhomlaau led to a shift in his leadership style. He began to prioritise diplomacy and open communication with the neighbouring town of Nhomlaau, rather than resorting to force and aggression. Tensions between the two communities gradually dissipated, and a sense of mutual understanding and respect began to develop. This transformation also had a positive impact on the people of Duomduom. They were able to learn from the resilience and compassion of the Nhomlaau people, which helped them grow and evolve as a community.

The once isolated and closed-off village now had a newfound sense of connection and camaraderie with its neighbours. This lesson would serve them well in the future as they navigated through the challenges of coexisting in a diverse and ever-changing world.

Chapter Twelve

After the reconciliation between Nhomlaau town and Duomduom village, the skies opened, blessing the earth with refreshing rain. The rain brought unity and togetherness as the townspeople joined in the joyful celebrations. The hostile atmosphere had dissipated, replaced with a warm one. The two communities had come together in a way that no one thought possible, and a newfound respect and admiration blossomed between former enemies.

As the rain eventually subsided, the sun emerged from behind the clouds, casting its radiant beams upon the two communities. The golden glow illuminated the once-dark landscape, symbolising the dawn of a new era. The people of Nhomlaau and Duomduom stood together, basking in the sun's gentle embrace, grateful for the new bond that had been forged. And as the sun continued to rise, so did the hopes and dreams of the two communities, united and stronger than ever before.

The next day in Duomduom village, the sun rose over the

horizon, casting its warm rays on the village square. The villagers were gathering to celebrate a long-awaited peace treaty between their two communities. It was as if a cloud of ignorance had been lifted, and the two communities were seeing each other for the first time. They were no longer strangers, but neighbours who shared the same land and the same dreams.

The colours of the sky shifted from deep purples to bright oranges. The laughter and chatter grew louder, filling the air with a sense of joy. It was a day that would be remembered for generations to come, a day when two worlds came together and united as one.

The villagers had been wary of the townspeople at first, their suspicion rooted in years of distrust and animosity between the two groups. As they interacted more, they were all just regular people trying to make a living and provide for their families. They shared stories, laughed together, and began to form a genuine connection. The townspeople admired the villagers' resilience and their ability to thrive despite their limited resources. It was a humbling experience for them, and they began to shed their prejudice to embrace their newfound friends.

Thereafter, the village of Duomduom became a place of celebration and laughter, with the townspeople visiting often and bringing gifts. The townspeople were welcomed with open arms, and the villagers were eager to share their culture and way of life.

It served as a reminder that despite their differences, they shared a common belief in the power of forgiveness and understanding. This lesson was etched into the minds and hearts of future generations, ensuring that the tale of Nhomlaau and Duomduom would be passed down for years to come. The two communities stood united under the same sky. From that day on, the two communities lived in harmony.

As the sun rose higher in the sky on the celebration day in

Duomduom, the people of both Nhomlaau and Duomduom gathered to witness this momentous occasion. They stood side by side, their differences forgotten, as they watched the two worlds merge.

The day after that celebration, the fruits of reconciliation manifested themselves. The villagers were in disbelief, their eyes wide with amazement as they watched the procession of trucks slowly make their way into the village. It was as if a miracle had occurred, bringing with it an abundance of nourishment that they had never seen before. The villagers couldn't contain their excitement and joy, as they rushed towards the trucks to get a closer look at the overflowing provisions.

Arriving at the outskirts of Duomduom village, the trucks came to a halt in a vast field adjacent to the residence of the Executive Chief of Duomduom village. The Executive Chief summoned the locals to offload the cargo. This simple task carried with it an unspoken weight, a reminder of the Chief's authority and the villagers' duty to serve.

As the villagers got to work, the Executive Chief watched on with a stoic expression. The cargo being unloaded was not just any ordinary goods, but rather a shipment of relief supplies for the villagers. These supplies were scarce, and the villagers were grateful for the Executive Chief's efforts in securing them.

The trucks were filled with bags of rice, wheat, and other grains, as well as fresh fruits and vegetables. Some of the villagers had tears in their eyes, as they had never experienced such an abundance of generosity. It was a beautiful and heartwarming scene.

With the conflict finally over, the villagers could begin to rebuild their shattered community and heal from the trauma they had endured. For the children of Duomduom, seeing the trucks filled with toys and school supplies was a moment of pure joy. Now, they could finally play and learn like any other child. The adults were grateful for the medical supplies that were brought, knowing that they could save countless lives. Their previously barren village was now brimming with life as people eagerly unpacked the supplies.

The vibrant, golden rays of the sun set over Duomduom, casting a warm glow over the bustling village below. As the villagers worked together to distribute the donations, they couldn't help but feel grateful to Nhomlaau for their generosity. The trucks were a symbol of hope for the future, offering them a chance to break free from the hardships they had endured for so long. The arrival of the trucks marked a turning point for Duomduom – it was the beginning of a new era, one filled with potential.

As the construction of new buildings and roads began, the villagers of Duomduom felt a renewed sense of hope and optimism. The infusion of energy and vigour in Duomduom was tangible. The villagers worked alongside the Nhomlaau inhabitants towards transforming Duomduom into a town. The once barren land was now filled with the sounds of construction and the sight of new buildings being erected. The villagers learnt a different way of life while sharing their customs and traditions. This exchange of cultures was enriching for both parties and created a stronger bond between the two worlds.

With every brick added to the construction, the villagers of Duomduom could see a brighter future on the horizon. The constant hammering and the smell of fresh cement in the air were a sign of progress. They found comfort and solace in the fact that their lives were changing for the better. The construction was not just about building physical structures; it was also about rebuilding their lives and their spirits. As the construction continued, so did their hope and determination to create a better world for themselves and their loved ones.

When the village was finally rebuilt, it was a bittersweet

experience. They were grateful to the people of Nhomlaau for their benevolence and for providing them with a new home, but they worried about the future for their children. They knew that the children would grow up without the resilience and fortitude that their ancestors had possessed. Without the harsh realities of life, the younger generation would not be able to develop the same level of grit and determination. The elders feared that this would make them ill-equipped to face the challenges of the world outside the village.

The village's reliance on Nhomlaau for its survival had created a power dynamic that was hard to ignore. The villagers were grateful for the help, but they also felt indebted and powerless. The elders recognised the need to empower the younger generation to become self-sufficient. The people of Nhomlaau had shown them great kindness, and it was their duty to repay that kindness by becoming productive members of society.

The villagers were determined to prove themselves and make their benefactors proud. The older generation had seen what the younger generation couldn't – the importance of hard work and self-sufficiency, lessons that the younger generation had failed to learn. Nhomlaau had provided for the village, but the older generation knew that this couldn't last forever. This village was built on the backs of its ancestors, who had toiled and struggled to make a life for themselves.

The younger generation, on the other hand, would live in a world of convenience. They would never know the struggles and hardships that their parents and grandparents had faced, and as a result, they would lack the resilience necessary. The divide between the two generations would be a source of tension in the village.

Despite the elders' concerns, the younger generation continued to live in blissful ignorance. To them, the people of Nhomlaau were heroes, providing for the village of Duomduom and allowing the villagers to live comfortably.

The Executive Chief, a man of great wisdom and foresight, recognised the need for a drastic change in the relationship between the two worlds. He called for a meeting between the leaders of Duomduom and Nhomlaau. During the meeting, the Executive Chief stated that he would be putting an end to Nhomlaau's provision of supplies to Duomduom.

The Executive Chief's reasoning was simple– he believed that by cutting off the supply of resources, the people of Duomduom would be forced to become self-reliant and, in turn, be motivated to help others in need. This decision was met with resistance from the leaders of Nhomlaau. However, the Executive Chief remained firm.

The Executive Chief argued that the current system was not sustainable and that by relying on Nhomlaau's supplies, Duomduom was limiting its own growth and development. He proposed a new way of living, one where the two worlds would be equal partners, trading with each other on a level playing field. The meeting ended without a clear resolution, but the seed had been planted.

The leaders of Nhomlaau understood that the decision made by the Executive Chief of Duomduom would open new avenues for trade and commerce. As a gesture of goodwill, they expressed their gratitude to the Chief and proposed an increase in trade between the two communities. The proposal to increase trade would not only benefit Nhomlaau but also the people of Duomduom.

With access to a broader range of goods, Nhomlaau would be able to improve its standard of living and enhance its economy. At the same time, the people of Duomduom would have the opportunity to market their goods in Nhomlaau, providing them with a new market and a chance to expand their businesses. This would create a win-win situation for both communities, further strengthening their ties. This would not only bring economic benefits, but also promote cultural exchange and understanding between the two communities.

The Executive Chief of Duomduom welcomed the idea.

Gutgook, the once fierce warrior, resurfaced once more. His presence was met with a mixture of nostalgia and admiration, as he reminded the people of a time when they were not just daydreamers, but doers. This time he took on the role of a mentor, urging the youth to toil diligently and break free from the cycle of waiting for handouts. He acknowledged the wisdom of the elders and humbly heeded their advice. Having already surpassed his fortieth year, he was now considered an elder himself.

Gutgook's message was powerful and inspiring. He spoke of a world where they were not merely victims of circumstance, but active agents for change. The youth were captivated by his words, their hearts brimming with a newfound sense of purpose. They began to see themselves as more than just poor villagers; they saw themselves as individuals capable of shaping their destiny. As they journeyed through the villages, Gutgook's words continued to resonate with them.

The youth's newfound determination was evident in the way they followed Gutgook. His words had opened their eyes to the possibilities that lay ahead. Carrying their tools with pride, the youth were ready to work towards a better future. They had been given a chance to break free from the constraints of their limited knowledge and explore the world outside their own. As they followed Gutgook, the youth realised that they were not alone in their journey. They had each other, and together they were stronger.

The youth toiled as a cohesive unit, tilling and reaping the land. The transformation was evident to all who saw them. The once demoralised youth now walked with their heads held high, their spirits lifted by Gutgook's guidance. The land was no longer barren and desolate, but instead flourished with the fruits of their labour. Gutgook had not only reminded them of their potential but also provided them with the tools and knowledge to fulfil it. Under his mentorship, the villagers had become a self-sufficient community.

The once-struggling economies of Nhomlaau and Duomduom were now flourishing, benefiting from the employment opportunities and bustling trade within these neighbouring villages. As the people of Duomduom found pride and joy in their hard work, the struggles of the past began to fade from memory.

The people of Nhomlaau and Duomduom also experienced a shift in their social dynamic. They began to see each other as equals, setting aside any previous prejudices or animosity. The passing of time had brought about a new era of prosperity and harmony for the once-divided villages of Nhomlaau and Duomduom. The two villages, once at odds with each other, had now become one. The people of Nhomlaau and Duomduom had put aside their differences and worked tirelessly to create a better world for themselves and their children.

As they looked back on their shared history, the people of Nhomlaau and Duomduom were filled with a sense of pride and accomplishment. They had overcome many obstacles and weathered numerous storms, but they had never lost sight of their goal: a brighter and more prosperous future. The passing of time had taught them that anything was possible when they worked towards a common goal, and they were determined to continue building a brighter future for themselves and their children. The tale of two worlds had now become a tale of unity, strength, and hope—an indication of the power of perseverance and the human spirit.

www.ingramcontent.com/pod-product-compliance
Lightning Source LLC
Chambersburg PA
CBHW010343170726
48283CB00009B/2931

* 9 7 8 1 7 6 4 2 1 9 3 4 1 *